The Second Pine Cone Collection

Randy Rogers

Other Books by Randy Rogers

The Pine Cone Collection

ISBN: 978-0-615-26236-9
Publisher: Lulu.com
Rights Owner: David Randall (Randy) Rogers
Copyright: © 2008
Language: English
Country: United States

In loving memory of my mother
Laura Nell Colvin Rogers

May she live on forever in my words

Acknowledgments

I think it was either me or Sally Field who once said, "Every actor needs a stage. Every writer needs a page."

What you're reading today would not have been possible without the help and encouragement of John and Susan Hays the publisher and editor of *The Morning Paper* in Ruston, Louisiana.

They gave me my (newspaper) page some years ago. I can never thank them enough for that.

Contents

Introduction

This book may seem a little bit more reflective than the last. It could have something to do with my turning fifty. I feel more nostalgic. Getting older has made me place more weight on what my friends and my memories mean to me.

One of my favorite stories in this collection is called "The Last Lap." Because none of us know whether we'll live to be 55 or 85, it's about not putting off until tomorrow what I can do today.

Thank you for taking the time to read *The Second Pine Cone Collection.*

Randy

Chapter One

Funny Business

Football Follies

It was great growing up during the Golden Age of football. I watched on TV as Vince Lombardi's Green Bay Packers defeated the Dallas Cowboys on the frozen tundra of the Ice Bowl.

Bart Starr ran a quarterback sneak to win it in the final seconds of a close and hard fought battle.

After that Sunday I was hooked. I started appending the words to Brother Doughty's closing prayer: "May the Lord bless you and keep you…and may the Saints beat the Falcons this afternoon, Amen."

I loved it when Joe Namath guaranteed, then delivered, a victory in Super Bowl III over the Baltimore Colts. He struck a blow for underdogs everywhere.

We did our best to emulate Broadway Joe and others like him in a field over beside Mark Moore's house. Almost every Saturday and Sunday afternoon during the fall and winter months you could pass that field and find it full of kids from Tatum's pond and other neighborhoods playing no-pads tackle football.

Unfortunately our public high school didn't have a football team. One year a private school opened up in town and offered the opportunity to play football with real uniforms and pads.

Some of us went over to give it a try. I found out straightaway how little I knew about the real game of football.

Our head football coach was Ronnie Fitzgerald. He had been a star quarterback at Bernice, La. and, although he enjoyed his job, he had trouble hiding his distaste for untrained football players. During our first practice, my conversation with Coach Fitzgerald went something like this:

Coach: Rogers, you'll play guard

Me: Right, which one is that?

Coach: Next to the tackle

Me: Right, which one is that?

Coach: Guard's next to the center. You do know which one is the center, right?

Me: He hikes the ball?

Coach: No, he *snaps* the ball

Me: Then who hikes it?

Coach: You do. I'm moving you to center

After a slow start, it didn't take us long to become one of the worst football teams ever to perform on the gridiron. We were small, but we were slow.

We were so bad Coach Fitzgerald said he couldn't even watch football on TV anymore. And you *know* you're on a bad team when opposing teams punt the ball back to you on their first down. Even then we couldn't score.

My cousin John Lane Norris was our quarterback. He was a gamer and gutsy as they come, but he might weigh 120 pounds holding a tire rim.

Our offensive line weighed just a little bit more but we couldn't stop John Lane from becoming a victim of mob violence.
Since our offense went backwards more often than forwards, my little cousin got creamed time after time and never complained. Just when I thought the last gang tackle got him, he would spring up, pull a clump of grass out of his face mask, and yell "Huddle Up!"

Hall of Fame linebacker Dick Butkus once joked that the first time he saw "Mean Joe" Greene of the Pittsburgh Steelers he knew he was tough because his socks were being held up by thumb tacks.

Our linebacker Jimmy Henry was that kinda tough. He'd gotten some experience playing football at Bernice and he used it regularly to beat us up in practice. He was so tough he once played in a game with his two broken hands protected only by knee pads and duct tape.

During one game, shortly after the opening kickoff, our assistant coach Bill Blaylock began running down the sideline screaming, "They've got a shotgun, they've got a shotgun!!" That meant the other team was going to run their offense from the "shotgun" formation.

Having never heard that football term before, I hid behind Jimmy Henry. If anybody decided to go nuts with a shotgun, I was going to be behind somebody I knew could stop bullets.

We learned early on that if you were the last one to get up from the pile the public address announcer would call out your name and say you were "in on the tackle." So I'd stay down and make sure I was the last one up.

I got busted one day by Coach Fitzgerald when he stopped me after a game and said, "Rogers, there's no way you had 42 tackles tonight."

By the time our winless season was over, not only could I name every position on the field, I had played most of them. Consequently, after I went back to public school that next year, I was a much better educated football fan.

To the Point

I'm not too sure when my septum first became deviated. I might have happened playing high school football. My helmet never fit right, and as Coach John Madden used to say, many times I got up from the pile looking out my ear hole.

It could have been a result of one of the vehicle wrecks I was in. Lord knows, I was in some good ones. Or maybe it was that time in a college bar in Baton Rouge when I told this drunken LSU linebacker to keep his hands off my date.

When I woke up, my nose felt deviated then.

I really don't care too much for that word deviated. It is just too close to deviant, as in behavior, to suit me. Like some neighbor would be calling Mama to rat me out for old times sake because she had observed my septum displaying deviate behavior.

"Larnell, you think that your son Randy would have the common decency to carry a handkerchief or use a Kleenex, but no, he sneezed in such a deviated fashion that, well, I simply felt obligated to call you and tell you about it. I know you'd do the same for me."

I've had problems with my nose for as long as I can remember. Congestion, drainage, sneezing, you name it, I've had it. I've seen lots of doctors and taken lots of antibiotics, but nothing seems to help.

First I went to an allergist who gave me a skin test. He said the problem was all in my head. Not a big fan of nose humor, I decided to go see an ear, nose, and throat doctor.

Dr. James Durante, my ENT, knows his way around the nose. He reviewed the results of my CT or CAT scan and called me in for a consultation.

Dr. D: Mr. Rogers, we've got your CAT scan back. Ha! Looks like you've got a Siamese…

Me: Is that nose humor? I'm not a big fan of…

Dr. D: Okay, right, let's get serious. The problems with your nose are nothing to sneeze at. The images of your sinus cavities are similar to that of a diseased Tibetan yak. Have you been to Tibet?

Me: Not since the war.

Dr. D: I'm recommending that we surgically remove your skull and…no, wait, that's at the autopsy. (flip, flip) Here it is.
Yes, I'm recommending that we go in, carefully scrape out your sinuses and pack your head full of painful gauze. While we're in there, we'll repair your deviated septum.

Me: How soon, do you think?

Dr. D: Well, certainly before someone calls your Mama

Not crazy about having any kind of surgery, I wanted to see if I could avoid it by scheduling a visit with Needles, my acupuncturist.

Needles is a Korean import who's set up shop over in Dallas. He can speak all of 10 words of English. We communicate mostly using his English dictionary, sign language, and grunts.

He has trouble saying Randy, so he calls me Yankee Dog. I call him Uncle Ho.

UH: Yankee Dog got snot, rots of snot.

Me: Grunt

UH: Rike Tibetan Yak. Yes?

Me. Grunt

UH: Been to Tibet, you?

Me: Not since war

UH: I fix nose. They no call Mamasan. Yes?

Me: Grunt. Yes, I guess…

So with the hope of avoiding my upcoming sinus surgery, I'm now taking Uncle Ho's acupuncture treatment and drinking his herbal tea twice a day. I sure hope it works.

Acupuncture's been around for over 2,500 years and it's proven in the past to be effective in treating the chronic pain I had in my neck and knee.

Both times I had very fine little needles inserted in my skin and then they were connected to an electric gadget that made them pulsate. As long as I close my eyes and think about something else, it's not as uncomfortable as you might think.

The only problem I have now is, whenever I let myself get too exited about something, my garage door goes up and down.

Randy No Handy

It's taken me years to come to grips with the fact that I'm not a born handyman. I'm not even adopted. In fact, I'd make Oliver Wendell Douglas on Green Acres look like Bob Vila.

Normally I try to put repair jobs off as long as I can, but recently I was forced to try my hand at plumbing. It was time. One of my toilets had become Old Faithful and its seat was starting to sound like a whoopee cushion. When it comes to going to the bathroom, I have just one simple requirement: The toilet needs to work. That's all.

I really don't care whether the seat is up or down. It's hinged to work both ways. Now I know some women who think it's a male character flaw to leave the seat up. I've always found that curious.

I'll tell you what I think really happened. One day they went in there and the seat was up and they fell in. Yep, then the word was spread around that some crude and inconsiderate Mr. Man was responsible.

Maybe that's where that deal about being madder than a wet hen got started too. Some hen went in, fell in, and got wet.

And that's also where hen pecking started. Hen went in, fell in, got wet, then went looking for some rooster to peck because of it. See how easily history can be explained? Hang with me, I'll make you smart.

Feeling that it's wrong for either gender to have to mop the floor after flushing or get credit for sounds they don't make, I set off to make the much needed repairs. As usual, I needed $200 in new tools to do a $40 job.

Since I've been banned for life from The Home Depot, I got my disguise down from the closet. I wear this ball cap pulled down over my ears and a fake mustache. It makes me look like the Unaplumber.

I made it past their greeter, who probably has my picture tucked somewhere in his orange apron, and headed for the plumbing supplies. I looked over the wide variety of Bemis toilet seats and picked out one that looked plenty wide enough. Then I made my way over to get one of those new fangled toilet tank doodaddies.

They don't have that copper ball inside the toilet anymore like they used to. Which is just fine with me because I could never get it adjusted right anyway. No matter which way I bent the bar or screwed the ball closer or further in it always kept the water too high or low.

The ones they have now have a space age thingamabob that slides down a pole when you flush sorta like that ball at midnight on Dick Clark's New Year's Rockin' Eve.

By the way, I caught Dick Clark on TV this past New Years. If I ever get like that, just shoot me and donate my remains to science. I'll thank you for it.
So now I'm home and I open up the box and get out the directions. Now let me ask you this. How much money does a company save by seeing how many languages they can cram onto one set of instructions? Invariably, I'm half way through with a project only to realize that I've been reading the instructions in German.

Did you know that "Wie komme ich dorhin?" translated into English means you dumbkoff, you got it upside down?

I finally got the new gizmo in the tank adjusted so that it drops down in true rockin' fashion and installed the nice new mouse-quiet throne seat.

Now if I'd really been thinking, I would have looked for a contraption that lowers the toilet seat back down automatically. That way some mad wet hen would have no reason to hunt me down and peck me. Hey, maybe that's where hunt-and-peck came from!

See? Hang with me, I'll make you smart…

Ghost Writer

Well you may have noticed that I missed having an article run in last week's paper. My brother Ben called wanting to get the results of the lab test. I told him there was no test; that I haven't even been to the doctor. I was just late turning the piece in.

The truth is, between my day job and managing the distribution of my new highly-acclaimed book, *The Pine Cone Collection*, finding time to write has been harder to come by.

That's the bad news. The good new is that the new book reviews are in and they are so good they're worth sharing with you. Here's the unedited version of what my loyal readers had to say:

"I laughed and cried"...first when I heard you wrote it, then when I heard you wanted 20 bucks for it." John Ed Colvin

"It's laugh-out-loud funny"...that you, who took English-as-a-second-language at LSU, have the nerve to write a book! Jim Rogers

"Author Randy Rogers is the next Lewis Grizzard"...and his new book is just as dead. Terry "T-Bone" Presley

"Couldn't put it down"...fast enough to make it to the bathroom to throw up." Billy Don Knowles

"The *Pine Cone Collection* breaks new ground"...and should be buried there as soon as possible." The library systems of America

Other than being dead and all, I wish I *was* the next Lewis Grizzard. He's my all-time favorite writer. He wrote classics like *Shoot Low, Boys - They're Ridin' Shetland Ponies and, Elvis Is Dead and I Don't Feel So Good Myself*

I know Lewis' book titles make mine sound a little dull, but it's only because my printer imposed a maximum four word title. You'd think I was sending a Western Union telegram. *The Pine Cone Collection* [stop].

Since Lewis had to meet a deadline for the *Atlanta Journal-Constitution,* I'm sure he faced many of the same challenges I have today trying to find the time and new ideas to write about.

I wish that I had been given the opportunity to meet Lewis before he passed on in 1994. It's like that joke about the beauty pageant contestant who was asked by the emcee, "If you could have dinner with anyone living or dead, who would it be?"

"Living," she said.

Besides the usual cast of historical figures to have at my dinner table, Jesus, Jefferson, Gandhi, et al, because we're birds of a feather so to speak, I think most of my questions would be reserved for Mr. Grizzard.

Our conversation might go something like this.

Me: Hey, Lewis. Glad you could come. It's good to see you.

L.G.: You can't see me, I'm a ghost.

Me: I know. It was just a figure of speech, I, uh…

L.G.: You're still writing for the *Morning Paper*? Making any money?

Me: Sure, well sorta. I get an annual subscription, good for $20 bucks a year.

L.G.: In other words, Hays is still throwing nickels around like manhole covers?

Me: You said it, I didn't. Hey, what sort of things did you keep in mind when you were writing your columns?

L.G.: First of all, writing a newspaper column is like being married to a Nymphomaniac. The first couple of weeks, it's fun.

But seriously, you're getting stuck sometimes writing, huh? Try doing what I did: sit down at the keyboard and wait for the blood to pop out of your forehead.

Me: Hmm, kinda graphic, but okay. Lewis, what do you think I could do to improve my writing?

L.G.: Well, if I were you, I'd first take a couple of weeks off, you know, just to relax.

Me: Relax. Okay, then what?

L.G.: Then I'd quit.

Me: Lewis, before you go, do you have a question for me?

L.G.: Yeah. What's up with Gandhi? He don't eat much.

Whether it's laughter or tears, it's a gift to be able to write something that stirs a reader's emotions. Lewis Grizzard had that gift.

Not too long ago, my two sweet cousins Ramona Wilson and Lisa Jane nee Colvin each sent me a nice note to tell me how they both laughed and cried while reading my book.

If it's not for the same reasons John Ed cited in his book review, I'll be happy to take that compliment and run.

Guy Walks into a Doctor's Office

I don't mean any disrespect, but sometimes I think the term M.D. may have once stood for mentally deficient. Probably that was before the AMA got together and unanimously voted to change it.

The pharmaceutical industry isn't much better. I think they're borderline nuts too. I concluded this when they started those verbal warnings in their TV ads about what to do when the benefits of Viagra last more than four hours. Am I really supposed to consult my physician? Right, I can hardly get in to see him now.

If I could get him on the phone though he'd probably prescribe that I light a couple of scented candles, get out the Silly String, and go for the Guinness Book or World Records. That is, of course, if there is a category for that sort of thing.

Then let's say they came out with Viagra for women. Should I call 9-1-1 if it sounds like my upstairs neighbor's been beating his wife for more than four hours?

If the police came to investigate and it was a false alarm, would that make him want his power saw back? See what I mean? Things like this bug me to no end.

I know this is starting to sound like a Jerry Seinfeld routine, but hey, I'm on a roll. Hang with me for just a little while longer.

Back on the subject of drugs, why do their names have to be so cryptic? Why can't they give them an easy name I can remember? If my blood pressure medicine was called Pump Magic I could remember that or maybe Sweet & Low for my blood sugar – same deal.

They should pay me to come up with some of the drug names. By George, I'll bet I could come up with some better names and they wouldn't have a single x, z, or y in them either.

Instead of just flipping through my chart and asking me if I'm still taking 20 milligrams of hyponitroximorphineclide, my doctor could just hold up a flash card with a picture of some pills and ask me, "You still taking these pills I gave you last time in the same amount and at the same time of day I told you to take them?" That would get an easier yep out of me!

I think the whole medical industry could use a mild laxative. I know my family doctor could use a hug today. He takes things way too seriously. I try to make him laugh every time I go in. Sometimes it works, sometimes it doesn't.

On my last visit, just to see if he was paying attention, I slipped a few tries into our normal (boring) conversation:

Doc: (Looking down at my chart) Are you allergic to any medications?

Me: Yes cyanide. Oh, and cobra venom. Uh, Rat poison too, but not nearly as much since my mother-in-law passed. Need some more?

Doc: What? No, that's good. (Flip…flip, scribble…scribble). So what seems to be the problem?

Me: Well, thanks to the Google God, I think I've got it narrowed down to either Malaria or Legionnaire's Disease. Which one of those do you consider more curable?

Doc: Depends, usually we treat the one that's covered by your insurance. One problem though I can see right off the bat is that, well, you're fat

Me: I think I need a second opinion

Doc: Okay, you're ugly too. So tell me, what happened to the nutritionist I referred you to? Did you eat him?

Me: Gunter? Nah, turned out he was a Nazi with an eating disorder

Doc: Shame it wasn't contagious…(Flip…flip, scribble…scribble)

Me: Doc, did I tell you my brother thinks he's a chicken?

Doc: Really? Why don't you have him committed?

Me: I would, but we need the eggs

Doc: Oh, did I tell you about the guy that came in yesterday with a bad rash on his arm?

Me: No

Doc: I examined the rash and asked him what he did for a living. He said he gave enemas to the circus elephants. I told him that was definitely causing his rash and that he should seriously consider seeking another profession.

Me: What did he say?

Doc: He said, "What, and leave SHOW BUSINESS?"

Me: Dang Doc. That was a good one!

Doc: Thanks! Hey, you've been a great patient. I'm here all week, except for golf on Thursdays. And on your way out, you be sure and tip your nurse. She's been working real hard for ya.

Dream On

Have you ever had a dream when you were sure it was caused by something you were watching before you went to sleep? I have. Especially when I was a kid, I'd get nightmares if I watched a scary movie before I went to bed. I would see that same monster again in my dream and wake up running away from it.

Now I think I'm starting to have dreams related to what I've had to eat. No kidding, the other night I fixed dinner with all the things I love to eat - good down home Southern stuff, the kinds of things that I've enjoyed eating all my life.

Then I had a dream that was a tad bit on the bizarre side. It seems that I was in the intensive care unit at Lincoln General in Ruston waiting to hear the results of my lab test. I'm in the bed when my doctor, Alan Herbert, walks in. Not today's version, but a younger Dr. Herbert - how he looked when he and Mama worked together – tall, big handlebar mustache and all.

He's got the chart in his hand and he's flipping through it and studying each page. I'm understandably apprehensive and studying his face for any hint of what news might be coming.

After what seemed like an eternity he put the chart down, sat down on the foot of my bed and started a conversation that went something like this:

Dr. Herbert: Randy, I want you to get a hold of yourself, now. We got some rough water to go through. If you can, I need you to relax and just listen to what I have to tell you. Can you do that?

Me: Yes, don't sugar coat it Doc. Give it to me straight. Is it the Big C?

Dr. Herbert: Yes, I'm afraid it is. It's cornbread…

Me: Dang! I knew it….I was afraid of that…Wait, what? Cornbread?

Dr. Herbert: Yes, specifically hot water cornbread. And unfortunately, it's in an advanced stage. We'll need to run some more tests to see how far it's progressed. We may need to bring in a specialist.

Me: Aunt Jemima?

Dr. Herbert: No, Mildred Swift.

Me: The cooking lady from KNOE? She's still around? When I was a kid I used to love watching her show on TV.

Dr. Herbert: Well, no one has more experience treating cornbread-related cases of this type than Mildred. She can also help us look for various known contributors.

Me: Contributors?

Dr. Herbert: Yes, known cornbreadcinogens – black-eyed peas, greens with pepper sauce and 'nana puddin'? You must have seen the Surgeon General's warning label about that? It came out in the 60's…

Me. Yes, of course, but I ignored it like everybody else. I guess I was in deep fried denial. I just didn't think it would happen to me.

I thought I could quit any time I wanted. I first tried acupuncture - then the patch. I asked my wife to hide the cooking oil and corn meal, but I'd just sneak out and buy some more or bum some from one of my neighbors. Nothing seemed to work. I was a slave to my addiction. And now it's come to this.

Dr. Herbert: But there is hope. As long as you never used butter or ketchup on your fried cornbread, with the proper treatment, the odds will be in our favor that you can experience a full recovery.

Me: Huh, really? Okay, then let's do this: Please tell Ms. Swift that we'll get back to her. Is Brother Doughty still waiting out in the hall? He is? Good, could you ask him to step in? I think it's time to administer last rites.

Invest This

The good news is, I'm only 14 years away from retirement. The bad news is, according to my calculations, I need 40 more quality earning years to be able to retire comfortably. I know comfortable is a relative term, but since I don't have any rich relatives who would feel comfortable leaving me their possessions, I'm going to say comfortable is my having enough money to keep the water running to my one-bed used travel trailer.

The most heavily weighted component in my investment portfolio, the Texas Lotto, let me down again last night. I bought five tickets and I didn't get one number right. I kept thinking I heard the TV show announcer say, "The fourth number is 27, another number Randy doesn't have. Hah! The next number is 12, (chuckle) he missed it again. He was close this time wasn't he? You had 21, right Randy?"

Over the years, I've gone through dozens of financial advisors but I'm trying out a new one now, Connie Cash, and I heard she's pretty good. She's the managing partner over at Cash & Burne, LLC and came highly recommended. I just hope those three letters don't stand for Lose Lotsa Cash.

I really hoped that we'd see eye-to-eye on my financial situation. It's not like I haven't tried to be a good steward with my money. It's just that me and money haven't had a chance to spend too much quality time together.

Prior to our first meeting, Connie asked me to bring along all my financial information so she could examine it thoroughly. She asked me about both my short and long term financial goals and explored what see called my "tolerance for risk."

Ms. Cash ended our meeting by saying that it might take a considerable amount of time to sift through all my financial information in order to put together a "comprehensive plan for meeting my financial goals." I could tell that she was a pro and understood my needs.

She worked fast. The following morning she called to tell me she was ready to have me drop back by her office to review her findings.

CC: Mr. Rogers, thanks for coming in, please have a seat. If you'll take a look at that document on the desk in front of you, you'll find that it contains our most current assessment of your retirement plans. Our firm's recommendation is explained clearly there in section IV.

Me: Hmm. It says here I should try and die at 65?

CC: Yes, if not sooner. Obviously except for your liver, we may be able to sell your other organs to cover your burial expenses.

Me: But what about my social security?

CC: Bankrupt. The Baby Boomers got it all

Me: What about my 401K?

CC: Well, that would have been helpful, but you invested in a 402K. Got that idea off the Internet did you?

Me: Well, the pop-up did say it was one better than a 401K? So I thought…

CC: And it said your rate of return was protected by the Crown Prince of Tonga? Didn't that set off any alarms?

Me: No. I have always had the utmost respect for royalty. Hey, by the way, what are my burial arrangements? Something tasteful I hope?

CC: Great Question. Do you still have your American Express card?

Me: I sure do. Both halves…

CC: Good then. Here's what you do: Glue your AMEX card back together and bring it in. At the time of your burial, we'll put it in your extended right hand and drive you in the ground with a mallet.

Me: What about perpetual care?

CC: Sure. We'll send someone over every now and then to weed eat and clip your fingernails

See You in the Funny Papers

My historically-famous but undocumented cousin, Will Rogers, once said he read eight different newspapers a day. When he was in a town with only one paper, he said he would read it eight times.

He would often read the daily newspaper aloud during his stage act because he said he could never come up with material that was funnier than what he could find in the daily news.

So let's give this a try. It's a late October Sunday morning here in Plano, Texas and the *Dallas Morning News* is out on the sidewalk. Before my sprinklers come on and turn it into papier-mâché, I'm going to go out and get the paper and see if I can relate to what my cousin Will was talking about. I'll be right back.

Okay here it is. I'll just flip through it to see if anything funny pops out…

It says here that some people at FEMA staged a press conference where their employees posed as members of the press. Well, it is getting close to Halloween and the only thing scarier would be to dress up as a member of FEMA. And FEMA? Puleeze, they were a fine group of impersonators to start with.

If FEMA had been managing the Titanic, not only would it not have struck an iceberg and sunk, it never would have sailed. I know some people in Louisiana who would trade FEMA for the Girl Scouts in a heartbeat. At least the Girl Scouts show up with cookies.

Okay moving on, it seems they've begun letting convicts out of prison in Southern California to fight those destructive wildfires. They'll get reduced sentences for their efforts. I guess that makes sense, provided none of them are arsonists.

Looks like the opinion polls have Hillary Clinton widening her lead over Barak Obama. From this photo, it looks likes she's been widening more than her base of support. If he wants back into the White House, I'd think somebody ought to tell her husband Bill to start hiding the Twinkie family-pak.

Oh, here's a good one! Louisiana Governor-elect Bobby Jindal said on CNN that his victory will put an end to the state's reputation for corruption and incompetence. Good for him!

But that does remind me of a scene from the movie Bananas where Woody Allen helps a Castro-like politician overthrow his government. To Woody's amazement, in his victory speech, the new leader tells the crowd, "We will now start wearing our underwear on the outside."

So you heard it here: if this new governor grows a bushy beard, starts wearing army fatigues and a beret, I'd advise the citizens of my home state to get out while they can!

Hmm, so now Britney Spears' old associates are suggesting that I boycott her new album "Blackout," but just until she gets her act together. Uh huh, well all right, they can count on me because: One, I'd have to be suffering from a blackout in the first place to buy her stuff. Two, you can't unburn toast.

That poor girl is just a couple of peanut butter and banana sandwiches away from being Fat Elvis. And it's sad that now mommy dearest has children? I pray for them. Not to sound mean, but that's one gene pool that should have been drained a long time ago.

What's this deal here about Iran, are we really thinking about attacking them? Oh wait, I just needed to read on some more.
It says the Admistration believes Iran may possess weapons of mass destruction. Boy, they're in trouble now! I just hope that we're sure this time.

Well, there doesn't seem to be that much more interesting to write about so I'll close by wondering what Will Rogers would have to say about this piece. I hope I didn't cause my dear near-cousin to roll over in his grave.

He was right you know. It is considerably easier to use the newspaper for material rather than write something from scratch. There are some things you just can't make up.

Let's Be Frank

A devoted female fan wrote me an e-mail the other day suggesting that my writing would be greatly improved if I would embellish it with more descriptive adjectives, adverbs, and some of the other terms I had to Google to see what they meant.

Personally, I always thought that style of writing was just one way of pumping up the word count so that my editor could fill more space between yard sale ads and the obituaries.

At first, I wanted to write her back and threaten to dangle a participle at her if she ever dared question my literary style again. But then I started thinking that she might be on to something, other than hard drugs, of course...

What would be the harm in modifying my writing style from time to time? Nothing I thought, so I decided to give it a try.

Here's how I write now:

> Frank set down on a damp park bench and got his butt wet. He ain't right.

That's 16 words. Along the lines of what my fan recommended, here's a more embellished version:

> It was a cold gray morning of a cold gray day in a cold gray city. Another day filled with abject loneliness and despair that only comes when one has lost the love of a lifetime.

> Frank sat alone on the edge of his bed contemplating whether this day would be different from any other.

> Through the dingy parted curtains and below the yellow pull-down shade he could see the park.

> Even the park looked cold and gray – so perfect for the mood that Frank was in, and so perfect for taking a walk.

> Thinking it might still be raining out, Frank grabbed his umbrella, the one with the two broken ribs. He should have parted with that umbrella years ago but it reminded him of happier days.

> He then made his way out the door and down the creaking wooden stairs that led to the street. He still walked with a slight limp courtesy of the Viet Cong mortar that landed too close to his foxhole. The years of physical therapy hadn't helped and he never went for his walk without downing three or more Advil caplets.

Frank preferred to take his walk in the early morning. He didn't need a watch to tell what time it was. He knew when the delivery van came by to drop bundled papers off by the newsstand that it was close to five a.m. Thirty minutes after that Jumbo Harry, the large goateed beret-wearing man, would arrive to unlock and raise the cover and awning to his street side stand.

Just like watching a baby being born, Frank loved to see the cold gray city come alive – ever so slowly, light by light, person by person until it was fully functioning.

That morning the sidewalk was empty. The park was empty, every bit as empty as Frank's life had become.

The wind was raw brisk and blowing in from the water as he walked along the lakeside sidewalk where the pigeons had begun to gather, waiting for the bread crumbs they knew he would bring. It was that way every morning, rain or shine, Frank leading his early morning marchers in a passionless parade.

As Frank neared the rusting green park bench he noticed that Carlos was already there. Carlos was a retired police officer who had trouble sleeping at night. He preferred the early mornings as well and would often keep Frank amused with stories from his cop days.

Frank said nothing as he sat down beside Carlos. He opened up his brown paper bag and began tossing bits of toasted bread on the ground around him.

Looking down and without making eye contact, Carlos asked Frank, "Did you know you just sat in some water?"

Uh huh, Frank mumbled.

"You ain't right, you know that? Carlos grunted.

Yep, Frank nodded.

So there, that wasn't so hard. I've learned a lot in this exercise and think this writing style might come in handy one day. Not that it's any great skill to be able to make a story go way longer than it should. I've known preachers and people at parties who could do that!

Fading To Blue

In the fall of 1979, I was quite proud that it only took me a little over five years to complete my four-year degree at Louisiana Tech. It wouldn't be long before I would have a diploma in my hand and be able to shop my 2.6 grade point average to the highest bidder.

I really didn't care what kind of job I landed so as long as it was legal, came with occasional toilet breaks, and had what most any civilized country would call air conditioning.

I went through the job placement center at Tech and had some interviews. I received a few job offers, but none like I wanted. One was with State Farm in Monroe; the other was with a life insurance company out of Dallas.

With my grade point average and my gift for gab they all figured I was cut out for sales. I couldn't disagree, I just wasn't too sure that I wanted to sell life insurance for a living.

My marketing professor, Dr. Holloway, called the apartment one day and asked me if I wanted to interview with IBM. Their local rep Glenna Feller, a Tech grad, had dropped by his office and mentioned that they had an opening for a territory sales rep in Shreveport.

Since my brother-in-law Ron Bringol worked for IBM, I knew that they were a top-notch group and that toilet breaks and air conditioning probably wouldn't be an issue.

I wore the same blue suit I was married in to my first interview, and the second, and the third. Finally the Branch Manager Jim "Red" Wood asked me, "Son, is that they only suit you own?" I said, yes sir, but if you'd hire me, I could afford to buy another one!

IBM offered me a sales job in their office products division selling typewriters, copiers, and dictation equipment. Just as I promised, I took my first paycheck into Lewis' Stag Shop and bought Big Blue's unofficial uniform - a dark suit, white shirt, conservative tie, and a pair of black wing tip shoes.

IBM's training program called for me to spend 12 weeks in the branch office. Back then they usually hired kids right out of college and taught them how to sell the "the IBM way." I watched videos, practiced my product demonstrations, and rode along on sales calls with the more experienced sales reps.

Nearing the end of my classroom training, Red called me into his office. He asked me to come over and stand with him next to a big map he had on the wall. "Son, I'm going to put you in Texarkana. Have you ever been there?" No sir, I responded. "Well, it's a fine territory; you'll like it up there, any questions?"

I shook my head. I'd been tipped off that Mr. Wood didn't like a lot of questions from rookie sales reps. Rather than ask him, I asked one of the senior reps what he knew about Texarkana. He asked me this strange question: "Do you bowl?"

I responded, bowl!? No. Well, hardly ever, why…?

"Oh, nothing… I think they bowl a lot up there," he said.

Now I don't have anything against bowlers. Their league shirts look comfortable. And just because I throw gutter balls and can never rent shoes that fit, that doesn't mean that I should jump to conclusions about the inhabitants of an entire city.

Actually it wasn't all that bad. A couple of years after I moved there some Yankee magazine ranked Texarkana the seventh worst city in the United States. Some of the natives were riled up and saying that that ranking was an insult. I agreed because Texarkana should have been ranked at least the SIXTH worst city in the U.S.

I ended up living in Texarkana for 5 years and worked for IBM up until they decided to dissolve our office products division. That was shortly after they introduced something called the IBM PC.

I thought I'd had the last laugh though. I moved away thinking: "Ha! Who in the world would want, much less need, a personal computer?"

And it's that kind of forward thinking that's made me who I am today.

Road Trip!

I've been doing a lot of traveling lately; making trips from Dallas over to Ruston, then down to South Louisiana - Lafayette, and New Orleans.

Mostly family business, but, as usual, I found a way to enjoy myself while I putting a few open road miles on the little gray Honda.

I can always tell when I'm back in the southern half of my native state; little things give it away:

First those little black love bugs start showing up and do the second best thing they do which is to smear my windshield.

Then the humidity makes my pores open up so wide I can almost see bone.

Lastly, when I stop for gas in Cajun Country, the pump display asks, "Raaan-DAY?? You want a receipt for dat gas, yeah?"

Unless you admire the majestic splendor of black gumbo mud, gnarled scrub oaks and mesquite trees, you'll agree with me that Dallas is every bit as pretty as a bowling shoe.

So when I get the opportunity to drive through South Louisiana, I let my eyes soak in all the sights - murky swamp water, cypress trees, and hanging moss. I call it getting my Louisiana fix, one I can take back home with me.

I first had the opportunity to experience that part of the state when I attended LSU in the early 70's. When the instructor called role in my first speech class and every other last name ended with a u or an x I knew I was living in a different kind of place.

It took me a while before I was able to pronounce some Cajun names correctly. I knew most of the easy ones like LeDoux, Hebert, and Robicheaux. Some were harder to pronounce.

I went into a Baton Rouge Burger King one day and the lady behind the counter asked me if I wanted "Mya-nez" on my hamburger. I was only eighteen, but I never thought I'd get stumped at a fast food restaurant. I had no idea she was referring to mayonnaise.

Once I decided to skip a semester at LSU and worked for Ledet (pronounced Li-DAY) Insurance Agency in Houma, Louisiana.. I pulled an insurance file for a gentleman who wanted to reinsure his shrimp boat.

The name on the file tab read "Authement." So I sat down across him at my desk and asked, So, Mr. Auth-MENT, how may I help you?

He looked at me a little constipated and then leaned over the desk and whispered: "Padnah, where you from…and, more importantly, how much longer you plan on staying 'round here?"

Well, at least till school starts back, I said.

"Then don't you think you better start learning how to pronounce the names right? Mine's OH-Dee-Ma, not AUTH-MENT, got dat?"

From that day on, I'd starting running those names past the office manager before I met with the customer. I thought it only fair that the locals should expect us Yankees from way up in North Louisiana to take some time to understand their language and culture.

We once had this politician in Louisiana with the most beautiful sounding French name: Camille Gravelle (pronounced Ka-MEAL Gra-VELL). One day I was watching the news on TV when the newscaster, obviously not from these parts either, said, "Today, Louisiana Secretary of State, Camel Gravel…"

Ha. I may have mispronounced a few French names, but I never called anybody camel rocks.

Before I crawled out of out of Baton Rouge on academic probation, forever ruining my chances of becoming a brain surgeon, I came to admire and appreciate the Cajun's outlook on life.

The French saying, laissez les bon temps roulette, or let the good times roll, means that you should live your life like you're dying tomorrow. If you've ever been to a Cajun funeral, you'd think you'd stumbled on a crawfish boil by mistake. They'll tell you that they'd much prefer to celebrate your life than mourn your death.

That makes sense to me.

So, I'm making this my new motto: Laissez les bon temps roulette, Raaan-DAY!!

Rent-a-Crisis

All I wanted was a rental car, nothing fancy, nothing flashy, just one that got good gas mileage and could get me safely to Nashville and back. My local Avis dealer recently changed hands and all the people I used to deal with there have moved on to become brain surgeons.

I guess they took my renter's profile with them, because this time, when I showed up to pick up my car, the transaction went something like this:

Avis: Mr. Rogers, we want you to know that we've taken the liberty of upgrading you free of charge. Here are the keys to a brand new Ford Mustang GT. It's parked right outside. Enjoy!

Me: A whut? I don't know if I should...what kinda gas mileage does it...? Don't the police pull over...That it, the red one over there? Wow. That's a nice lookin' ride. Okay, what the heck, live a little, right? I'll take it!

It's been a long time since I was behind the wheel of a car that, when you gave it some gas, it went vroom. My little gray Honda Civic doesn't go vroom. It sorta puts out this anemic high-pitched sound like a Singer sewing machine that needs a drop or two of oil.

But this Mustang had vroom to spare. That sound brought back fond memories of the muscle car I owned in high school. With its Hurst stick shift, four-on-the-floor transmission, dual exhaust with the cherry bomb glass packs, chrome tailpipe extensions, wide white-lettered tires, my baby blue and white 1969 Buick 400 GS could go take me from zero to dripping sweat in less than 6 seconds.

I've never owned a Mustang, much less driven one like this. When I sat down in the bucket seat, I felt like I was Steve McQueen in Bullitt. I was an impressionable 12 or 13 year-old when I first saw that movie at the Dixie Theater in Ruston.

In it, McQueen drove his 1968 Mustang GT at high speeds up and down the hills of San Francisco in pursuit of a black Dodge Charger. Most movie goers agree that it's one of the best car chase scenes of all time. If you don't believe me, you can check it out on YouTube.

I had almost everything I needed to complete the driving experience. I had my sun glasses. What I didn't have was a pair of black leather driving gloves. I stopped by Target on the way out of town to look for some, but I couldn't find any that didn't cut off the blood flow to my fingers.

Then I remembered that Steve McQueen didn't have the driving gloves, it was the guy driving the black Charger. So that made it okay for me to proceed on to Nashville carrying a clear cinematic conscience.

I made it all the way to Nashville without incident. After attending my meeting, I was headed up to Chattanooga to spend the weekend with by best friend Terry "T-Bone" Presley and his lovely wife Linda when I noticed the blue and red flashing lights in my rear view mirror.

I can't remember the last time I was pulled over. I thought it might be an emergency vehicle trying to get by so I pulled off onto the road shoulder as did the white county police vehicle behind me.

The officer was cordial enough. Our conversation went like this:

Officer: Good afternoon, sir. Nice car. Let me guess, Steve McQueen in Bullitt? Were you doing 80 chasing a black Charger?

Me: Well…not exactly, officer…I…

Officer: You know, that's my grandfather's favorite movie.

Me: Really, is it? That's nice. Is he still alive?

Officer: No sir. May I see your driver's license and rental agreement?

Me: Certainly. But how did you know it was a rental car?

Officer: You're kidding, right sir? Middle-aged man in red Mustang GT, did you have trouble finding a pair of black leather driving gloves?

Me. Well I tried, but I couldn't find any that fit and…you know, that was the guy in the black Charger who had the gloves…not …

Officer: Yes sir. That's what Gramps said. Would you please remain in your vehicle while I check to see what all you're wanted for?

So, with the first and only speeding ticket I've ever gotten, I drove my red rented middle-aged man-toy back to the Avis lot.

The new owner was there to check me back in. "Mr. Rogers, I know you rented your cars from the previous owners and I just want to thank you personally for continuing to do business with us. I hope you'll accept a small gift as a token of our appreciation."

"Well now, how nice, thank you very much. What is it?"

"It's a pair of black leather driving gloves. I hope we have your correct size."

Phone!

Although it was never for me, when the kids still lived at home, the phone rang all the time. Well, I'll take that back. Occasionally an assistant principal would call, but never to tell me what a joy my sons were to teach or how they had made the honor roll (again) and how the other students were getting jealous.

I guess my school tax dollars didn't go to fund that activity.

Like me, my sons, William Brian Rogers and Michael Brady Rogers, go by their middle names. So I knew it wasn't going to be a parent's proudest moment when the phone rang and the conversation started off: "Uh, Mr. Rogers? This is the assistant principal over here at the middle school? Yes sir, I'm calling to talk to you about your uh, son, (flip, flip) uh, William?"

I wish now that I'd had thought of something clever to say, something that could have injected a little humor into what clearly was going to be bad news?

Maybe I could have said: "Yes, thank you for calling. This is his father, David. Are you calling about his sex change operation? It's scheduled a week from Thursday."

"No? Then has he, well she, made the honor roll (again) thereby making the other kids jealous? Either way, let me begin by saying how thrilled I am to see how my school tax dollars are being spent. I'm so sorry to interrupt, please continue…"

Now that the boys are grown and gone, the phone hardly rings at all. Lately it's been a recording telling me that the warranty on a car I don't own is about to expire. Either that or it's a political message telling me the world will go to hell in a handbag if I don't send money in to one candidate or another.

I wish having a phone wasn't a necessity these days. When I was a kid, my folks believed the phone was for emergencies-only like the hotline to the Kremlin.

They told me that talking to my girlfriend meant that a neighbor couldn't call to tell us that our house was on fire. Ha, like we wouldn't smell the smoke?!

If it wasn't for the negative financial impact it would have on the telemarketing community and ruin the entertainment value they bring me I would have my home phone disconnected.

I actually enjoy getting calls from telemarketers. I'd add my name to the "Do Call List" if there was one. Whenever they call, I do my best to see if I can get them off their appointed mission.

Telemarketer: Good afternoon sir, is your wife home?

Me: Are you with the police?

Telemarketer: No sir.

Me: Have they located the body yet? I hid it pretty good, didn't I?

Telemarketer: I uh, sir, I don't know, I'm calling from...

Me: Can you take my confession over the phone, or will I need to come down to the station?

Telemarketer: No, I uh, mumble, [click]

When it comes to dealing with telemarketers, I play the game of opposites. If they're looking for married people, I say I'm single. If they want to sell me renter's insurance, I own. Clean my carpet? Nah, sorry, I've got wood flooring.

Sometimes I tell them I have to let my (imaginary) little brother Nicky do that job to help pay for his daughter's speech therapy. "Bless her little heart. Couple more lessons and she'll be able to say Philadelphia without spitting."

Not many of them seemed very touched.

You can always tell when it's a telemarketer calling because there's this short pause between the time you say hello and when they come on the phone. That lets me I know it's a good time to use this language I made up.

After their first question, I'll blabber along and say "Que" every so often, which I'm pretty sure means "what?" in Spanish. That's to make them think it's a bona fide language. I'll keep on speaking gibberish until they hang up.

I had one phone guy so frustrated he practically yelled, "Doesn't anyone there speak English?" With my best British accent, I responded, "No, sorry mate," and hung up.

Ha! Can you hear me now?

You Don't Say

The last time I was home, I ran into Ms. Sue Moore at Starbucks. She was with her daughter Becky, and her lovely granddaughter Amanda. I told Ms. Sue that I was almost finished writing a column about the bridge club she and Mama used to belong to. She was one of Mama's closest friends and an avid bridge player.

She said, "Please don't tell everything," and we both laughed. I get that request quite often.

I don't know if they still do, but the NY Times' banner used to read, "All the news that's fit to print." Well, half of the time what I hear, I can't print. When I'm back home, I love going to the coffee shop on the hill in Dubach and listening to the Council of Elders at the back table at Campbell's One Stop. But the majority of things I hear are a little low on the repeatability scale, if you know what I mean.

Bill Pendergrass, my favorite Lincoln Parish storyteller, will occasionally give me a quotable quote. Like the other day when I asked him if he thought Bobby Jindal was really going to be able to clean up Louisiana politics.

He said, "Sure, but I'm just afraid we're gonna lose our number one place in corruption. You know, we've been leading in the polls forever, all the way back to the Huey Long days. If Jindal has his way, that could ruin our reputation. We could fall as far as fourth place, right behind Mississippi. Holy freezer money! Wouldn't that be a tragedy?"

Bill said there was still hope, though. "If we can ever get our ex-governor out of federal prison and back in the game, we could reclaim our position in no time!"

Assuming Bill was referring to our former governor Edwin "It-ain't-stealing-if-you-don't-get-caught" Edwards, I'm thinking he's a little long in the tooth to be leading the Bayou Baksheesh Boys back to victory. At his age, could you imagine him trying to negotiate with a modern day bribest?

Bribist: Governor Edwards, I have an envelope here for you from FOG, the Friends of Gaming? You remember how you helped us get into your state?

The Gov: Who? Boggs? Hale? Naw man, he's dead.

Bribist: No, Governor, not Hale Boggs. FOG, FOG, Governor. Are you having a problem with concentration?

The Gov: Huh? Naw, I went this morning…good one too.

I know there are things you don't say on airplane, but just one day, I'd love to have a conversation with a flight attendant that went like this:

Me: Can I smoke on this plane?
FA: No

Me: But it's okay to smoke in the lavatory as long as I dismantle the smoke detector. I wouldn't be subject to a fine or imprisonment, right?

FA: No and yes.

Me: Am I free to get up and move about the cabin if the seat belt light is on?

FA: No

Me: What about the whole "prepare for cross check" thing ya'll do?

FA: What about it?

Me: Do you think Jesus performed the first cross check?

FA: What? Sir, don't you think you're being a little sacrilegious?

Me: Well, probably, but I'm curious. Do you think Jesus looked left and right and said, "Yep, we're good to go?"

FA: Sir, I find that humor in very poor taste

Me: Like your pretzels?

FA: Well, yes

I believe that one day I'll be standing at the pearly gates before St. Peter and have some explaining to do.

I can see him flipping through the Book of Rogers and saying, "Hmm. Let's see here: Salesman, newspaper columnist, probably had to bend the truth a little, but we can look past all that."

"Baptist who drank a bit, but hid it well... Yep, that's okay. We've got a lot of those here. I don't see anything here in the book that would prohibit you from getting into heav... Uh oh, wait, hold the phone, did you write a piece about Jesus performing the first cross check?"

Chapter Two

Of God & Country

A Marine Comes Home

It was harder this time, watching him come home from the war.

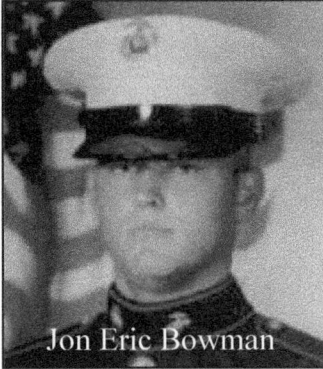
Jon Eric Bowman

His stepping off the bus was not a given. Another local boy, another U.S. Marine, Jon Eric Bowman had not made it home. He lost his life in Ar Ramadi 9 October, 2006.

She knew Jon Eric and his family. While it was best for her sanity to put the notion aside, she knew that once you send a son into harm's way there's a chance you might become another gold star mother.

This was one of those times that only seeing him, holding him, would be enough to convince a mother that her son was really back from his second tour.

I asked my sweet little cousin, Lisa Jane Whitard, to tell me more about how she felt the day her Marine son Jared stepped off that bus. I'm sure she didn't expect what she wrote me to wind up in print, but I thought she could tell this story much better than me:

"I think it was harder this time because, after seeing Jill lose Jon Eric, I realized how unbelievably blessed we were to be getting him home okay. If you've never witnessed first hand a parent losing a child you can be oblivious. It's impossible when you've seen it first hand. If you want to know about feelings - indescribable joy!!!! It rivaled giving birth to him - actually, I think it surpassed it."

"If you sat and looked around at all of the families you would see a range of emotions...nervousness, anxiety, excitement, but nothing like the excitement and the exhilaration on everyone's face when we were finally told the bus was almost there."

"I'm telling you Randy, there was nothing like it. I didn't notice anyone else until after I'd gotten my hands on Jared. Then when I finally noticed other families, there was laughter and a WHOLE lot of tears.

I happened to glance behind where we were standing and there was a Marine holding a newborn - two months at the most.

He couldn't take his eyes off of him. It was his son, and he was just getting to meet him. Yep...you guessed it - I squalled!!!!!"

"The unit was plastered with Welcome Home signs, yellow ribbons, and more American flags than you could count. When they arrived at the airport, they were escorted all the way to the unit by a police motorcycle escort. The two major TV stations in Jackson were there."

What can one say about those like Jared who have answered their country's call not once, but twice? How could you thank a mother enough for giving him that emotional permission slip to go and serve where and when he was needed?

When some friends of mine in the reserves and National Guard were getting called up after 9-11, I wrote a lyric about a soldier who had to leave his family behind.

I never got around to writing the chorus, but here are some of the lines I dusted off.

It's called "On the Line."

> Packed my duffle bag and do rags
> Hear things have gotten rough
> I got my orders today
> They've called my unit up
> I'm shipping out in a day or two
> I wish I had more time
> My country's got some fighting to do
> And they want me on the line
>
> Knew this might happen soon
> Ain't nobody's fool
> Nobody ever drafted me
> To do what I have to do
> Before I enlisted

I had college on my mind
Now my country's got some fighting to do
And they want me on the line

Calm your fears, dry your tears
One day, one day, I'm coming back
Then we're gonna pick right up
Before there was Iraq
A husband and a father
Got to leave you all behind
'Cause my country's got some fighting to do
And they want me on the line

When Johnny Comes Marching Home (Again)

When I was a kid, it was Viet Nam, a jungle and rice paddy war being fought way over there by almost nobody I knew. Once voted the most trusted man in America, Walter Cronkite and the CBS Evening News provided the grainy images of wounded soldiers being carried on stretchers to waiting helicopters.

That was usually followed by a graphic scoreboard that indicated how many enemy troops had been reported killed or captured versus our side. Their number was almost always higher than ours and that helped us to believe we were winning the war.

Then one day we saw images of helicopters being shoved off an aircraft carrier into the South China Sea and thousands of refugees fleeing their capital city holding just what they could carry on their backs. Then the tanks rolled in, the enemy hoisted their flag, and it was over. Only wars are never over, they live on in the men and women who fight them.

I've known a lot of warriors in my life. All were affected by what they saw. In a very small way I can relate. As a 21 year-old deputy sheriff, I saw people who had been shot and killed. I had the hardest time getting used to the idea there were people out there who would hurt me because of the uniform I was wearing.

Even with the proper training, death is not an easy thing for a 19 or 20 year-old to face. Terror and sadness have a way of taking a toll on a body and mind. So you can do your job, there's a numbing process that takes place. Medical people call it becoming "clinical," meaning if they broke down every time a patient expired they wouldn't last very long in their profession.

He's retired now, but thirty years ago, I asked Louisiana State Trooper Greg Gossler how it felt to work a car crash when young kids were hurt. He said 'I've got too much work to do at the time just working the wreck. It's usually after I get home, when it's quiet, that's when it hits me - what happened - and that's the toughest time.'

A friend of mine once told me that he had a brother who went off to fight in Viet Nam. When he came back, he wasn't the same person. He left as an outgoing, funny, always-smiling brother and came back a veteran who could not talk about his experience. He said he had trouble sleeping, drank a lot, and was somber and bitter. Most of the time he was staring off into space like he was looking into a portal no one else could see through. The guilt that our nation laid on some of those vets had a lot to do with how they coped after coming home - which was not well

When a warrior gets home, away from the battle and away from his buddies that is the toughest time. Who are they supposed to talk to? Who can relate to what they've been through? I know I can't. I don't know what it's like to hold a dying comrade in my arms, hear him with his last breath ask me to tell his mother or his wife that he loves her.

Walter Reed Hospital in D.C. and the Brooke Army Medical Center in San Antonio have many badly wounded warriors who will tell you they can't wait to get back to their units. Sure they miss the adrenaline of combat, but more than that they miss the esprit de corps that develops between men and women after the fighting starts.

It's when the fighting stops that they need us the most. Not to tell them that we know what they've been through, because we don't. Not really. They need to know that we do understand that things might never be the same; that the price they paid for our freedom may surely have cost them their innocence. We owe them that level of understanding and nothing less.

In the end, it's not the outcome of the war, but what comes out of the war, and how we handle it together, that matters the most.

The Golden Door

Friday was the 4th of July, America's birthday. Happy Birthday America!

It's been a long time since I've given much thought to the real meaning of this holiday. Like most Americans I guess that I'm guilty of thinking more about my having the day off or trying to decide what I'm going to grill that afternoon.

It's about time that I took the time to think about our country's birthday and what a truly special place America is.

Let me begin with the inscription at the base of the Statue of Liberty: It reads "Give me your tired, your poor, your huddled masses yearning to breathe free. Send these, the homeless tempest-tossed, to me. I lift my lamp beside the golden door."

America has always lifted her lamp beside the golden door to her tempest-tossed. Whether they came through Ellis Island or another historical point of entry, the tired the poor have always shown up at Lady Liberty's feet looking for the path to a better life.

Our nation's forefathers, who had seen tyranny and oppression in their time, decided to pen a document that stated that all men were created equal and endowed by our Creator certain inalienable rights.

Was it not this country that first constitutionally backed the desire of its citizens to have life, liberty, and the pursuit of happiness? Was it not that very promise that compelled so many to leave their homelands and cross open waters?

Expecting a different answer I'm sure, a reporter once asked outgoing British Prime Minister, Tony Blair, to sum up his opinion of America.

He said that you can best judge a country by seeing how many people want to get in versus out.

He's right you know. And I think that was seconded some years back by the great Yankee philosopher, Yogi Berra, who once said, "Nobody eats at that restaurant any more. The lines are too long."

Any true patriot would agree there's only one good reason a restaurant would have a long line.

By George Washington, it's because something inside is worth the wait!

When is the last time you read a news story about someone constructing a rickety craft so they could float from America *to* Cuba? I'll bet you a Cuban sandwich and a side order of black beans there's not a long line waiting to get into that country!

Other than the French who, as weird as it sounds, gave us the Statue of Liberty, most foreigners will tell you that, while they may detest our government's policies, very few of them hate the American people. That's because Americans give more than other nation to help the tired, the poor, the tsunami tossed of this world.

Why do Americans give so much? I guess it's because we can. We are a generous country. It's the American way to give to others in their time of need, and long before they ask.

Some countries even turn away our humanitarian aid lest their stricken countrymen embrace our generosity and lose their hate for America.

Americans are proud to serve. We serve at homeless shelters. Police officers are sworn to serve and protect. We serve in the military and on juries. People die every day in service to our country.

So this Fourth of July, my 52nd, was treated a little differently. It wasn't all about grilling hamburgers and enjoying a long weekend.

This Fourth, I took some time to reflect back upon why my ancestors came through the golden door of opportunity and how I am so very thankful they did.

Happy Birthday America!

To Return With Honor

Bob Peel

To look at him or talk to him, you wouldn't know that Bob Peel had anything to do with history.

He and his wife Chris are friends of mine, two very normal people, who gather at our local watering hole in Plano, Texas. He's a retired Southwest Airlines pilot. She works at the library.

Bob doesn't talk much about that day on 31 May, 1965 when he climbed into the cockpit of his F-105 Thunderchief and headed for a bombing run in the skies over North Vietnam. I doubt he ever stopped to consider that he might not be back for eight years.

In the Vietnamese language Hoa Loa means fiery furnace. That was the name of the miserable hell hole of a French-built prison where they took pilots like Major Robert Delayney Peel to be tortured and interrogated. They nicknamed it the Hanoi Hilton.

Although kept in isolation most of time, Bob was in some famous company. Now Senator John McCain was there as was former vice presidential candidate James Stockdale. Jeremiah Denton wrote a book about it titled, "When Hell was in Session." Bob's mentioned in most of the books. Ed Alverez was the first captured; Bob was the tenth.

Smitty Harris, Bob's buddy from Mississippi, developed a way of communicating among prisoners. It involved tapping on their cell walls. Somewhere along the line Smitty had learned that code in his survival training.

Different taps stood for the letters of the alphabet. Often times they would use this code to say comforting things to each other like "God bless you" or "good night, don't let the bed bugs bite." They could also discuss the arrival of new prisoners or which ones were being taken away for torture. No doubt their comradeship enabled them to prolong their individual breaking points.

It's hard to imagine how, but some found a way to keep their sense of humor. When someone would complain about their conditions, they might hear, "Well, if you don't like it, you shouldn't have joined."

When pressured by his North Vietnamese captors to tell them when he was born, one POW from Georgia wrote, "At an early age." When asked for his parent's name, he wrote "Mama and Daddy."

Not too long ago, Bob and Chris received a letter from a lady from Freemont, Wisconsin. Here's some of that letter:

> This may come as a surprise, as you do not know me. My name is Sally Hartfiel. As a young girl, my sister and I received POW bracelets. The bracelet I received was for Major Robert Peel.
>
> When I received the bracelet, I also was given your mother's address and I wrote to her. One letter from her said that she hoped one day I would grow up and marry with children and be able to tell my children the story of how the bracelet came to be.
>
> That letter still sits in our curio cabinet next to your bracelet and each time I read it, I cry. At twelve, I was so excited that my soldier was coming home. Your return was televised and I watched with pride as you exited the plane.
>
> I am so happy my daughter was able to locate you and your family, so that I could have the opportunity to share with you how much that bracelet means to me and my family. I want you to know how much we appreciate the extreme sacrifice you made for all Americans.

Bob was released 12 February, 1973. I too was watching on TV the day he got off the plane at Clark Air Force Base in the Philippines. Ed Alverez got off first. If they were able, they did their best to get off the plane in the same order they were captured. When they arrived, some got on their knees and kissed the ground.

Sometimes I think the Good Lord puts certain people like Bob in our path to remind us that our little inconveniences don't amount to much. When I stop to consider what he and his comrades went through in the fiery furnace, how they suffered, my not having enough hot water seems trivial and petty.

Their sworn goal was to return with honor, and they did. To all of those: God bless you. Good night, and don't let the bed bugs bite.

My Cousin, the Marine

In the framed photograph that sits on the counter behind her teller station, it's hard to tell who looks more proud, the squared-away Marine in his dress uniform or his mother standing next to him.

I've never met her Marine although I know he comes from good stock. He's part Pendergrass, which means he's probably quick-witted and funny. I've never known a Pendergrass who wasn't.

I enjoy stopping by to see his older cousin, Ty Pendergrass, at his office in Minden. Ty and I were running buddies in high school and he's always been my best source for finding out what's been going on lately in our hometown.

I wish you had a chance to meet the Marine's, late great granddaddy, Mr. Quedulous Pendergrass. He was a splendid piece of work and I'm guessing the original source of the Pendergrass family's ability to entertain.

Mr. Q.D. loved baseball. I never knew him to miss a baseball game he could get to. He even named his son, Ty's daddy, Tyrus Tristan Pendergrass, after two of the best players in baseball history - Ty Cobb and Tris Speaker.

Mr. Tyrus had been a really good ballplayer when he was at La. Tech. He also volunteered to coach me and Little Ty's baseball team one summer. Although he did his best, he didn't have much talent to work with and I seem to remember we lost more than we won.

The Marine's maternal uncle, Reagan Colvin, is one of the funniest story tellers in North Louisiana. He was a pretty fair baseball pitcher too! I remember one time, when Reagan and I were high school teammates; I got into a dispute with

Coach Howard Brown over his decision to move me back in the pitching rotation.

Insulted, I verbally floated the idea around the dugout that I should leave the team in protest. I asked Reagan, in a show of solidarity, if he would consider walking off the team with me. Reagan replied, "No, with you gone, I'll get to pitch more."

I understand that Reagan is preaching the gospel now, which is nice. I think it also says something about the Lord having a good sense of humor.

Reagan's oldest sister Ramona, or Mona Kay, as anyone who grew up in Dubach would still call her, is a certified hoot. I think she married John Lane Wilson shortly after she got her temporary driver's license.

She came back to our high school when I was a senior to do her student teaching. She asked us to please, please, call her Ms. Wilson in the classroom instead of Mona Kay. It was a hard habit to break, but since she was an old married lady and all by then, we cut her some slack.

Mona Kay's baby sister is Lisa Jane Whitard. She works at the bank in Dubach. Her son Jared Whitard is the Marine in the picture. He's now serving his second tour in Iraq.

I try to stop by the bank and visit with Lisa Jane every time I'm in town. She told me once that some of the stories I've written about people I knew who served in the military made her cry. Now I know why. They reminded her of Jared.

I can't imagine how it feels to see a loved one go off in harm's way. I asked Lisa Jane is she could one day write about that experience. She said maybe one day, but for now, the emotions are still too raw. I understand.

I also understand why Marines are special. I've got three very good friends who are former Marines – John Ciruti, John White, and Doug Champagne. I know now never to refer to them as ex-Marines. John Ciruti says there's no such thing as an ex-Marine. Once a Marine, always a Marine, right John?

So the cousin I've never met, Jared Whitard, part Colvin, part Pendergrass, all Marine, has again joined the long line of the few and the proud.

I hope that you'll join me in saying a prayer for his safe return and for all those who serve our country.

A Postcard from Texas

I think by now I've professed enough love for my native state of Louisiana that it's okay to say some nice things about my adopted state of Texas.

Although they didn't know each other at the time, my parents were the first ones of our immediate family to live in the Lone Star State. They both lived as kids in the Rio Grande Valley. My dad lived in Harlingen and my mother in Primera, Texas just a little wisp of a town 35 miles away.

Growing up I heard lots of stories about what it was to grow up in The Valley – walking around shoeless and swimming in irrigation canals on Christmas. Back then that area was a Garden of Eden capable of growing food year round.

My folks took me back there one hot mid 60's summer. I saw lemons as big as grapefruits and the little house where Mama lived. It still had the scrawny Mesquite tree by the front porch that Mama said she'd shinny up to get out of reach of Granny's whipping broom.

We didn't have a Mesquite tree back in Louisiana, but I had a similar maneuver. I used to crawl under the bed so Mama couldn't reach me with her belt. I had no idea that sort of thing was inherited. After I got a little older and bigger I couldn't fit under the bed anymore. This allowed Mama to make up for all those missed opportunities. One sure down side to growing up I'd say.

When Buddy Mercer and his family moved to Dubach from Dayton, Texas that was the first time I learned that Texans have their own category. Our kid conversation went something like this:

Me: Is Texas part of the South?

Buddy: What do you mean?

Me: You know, are you a Southerner?"

Buddy: I'm from Texas

Me: Yeah I know that but, do you consider yourself a Southerner?

Buddy: No. I'm from Texas, I'm a Texan

Although they fought on the right side of the War of Northern Aggression most native Texans see themselves as just that – Texans. Not Southern, not Western, just Texan and darn proud of it.

They even have a bumper sticker out here that reads "Native Texan." That's so you won't lump them in with the multitudes of carpet-bagging Yankees who have descended on their state like a biblical horde of horn-honking locusts.

I don't recall ever seeing a bumper sticker that read "Native Louisianan." Maybe that's because it would have so many letters and the print would be so small you might have a wreck trying to get close enough to read it. I've heard of that happening before.

When I travel, I don't like to say I'm in from Dallas. That's because Dallas still carries some negative baggage over the 1962 JFK assignation. I prefer to say I'm from Texas. That usually gets a more positive reaction.

People seem to like hearing that you're from Texas. I guess the word conjures up images of large ranches, long horned cattle, and horses. Everybody thinks we have a least one of those. Truth is, I don't even own a pair of cowboy boots much less own a horse or know how to ride one.

I remember a scene out of the TV series *M.A.S.H.* when Colonel Potter was looking in on a wounded U.S. soldier from Texas. He said something along the lines of, 'I've never known someone from Texas who didn't extend his hand first in welcome.'

Texans are indeed a friendly bunch.

My favorite show of all time is the made-for-TV saga *Lonesome Dove*. Even though he was born in San Diego, Robert Duvall was mighty convincing in his role as a former Texas Ranger Gus McCrae.

Even though he attended Harvard, so was Tommy Lee Jones, who after all is an eighth-generation West Texan.

To me, Texas is defined by the music of Willie Nelson, Lyle Lovett, Delbert McClinton, Don Henley, Guy Clark, and Bob Wills and the Texas Playboys.

It's the beauty of the hill country around Austin and the lazy river that snakes through San Antonio.

It's the smelly old honkytonks like Gruene Hall and the dance hall in Lukenbach.

Texans have a strong sense of independence and pride. They'll let you know historically that they were a republic before they were ever a state and that Texas has the right to secede or divide into as many as five separate states.

Given that potential to take their state and go any time they want, I know now how they came up with their state slogan:

"Don't mess with Texas"

Altered States

My sweet little cousin, Lisa Jane Whitard, nee Colvin, Marine Jared's mom, Mona Kay's and Reagan's baby sister, Alan's wife, etc. works at the bank in Dubach. The last time I stopped in to visit with her I happened to mention that I might be doing a book signing at the Bienville County Library in Arcadia.

Lisa Jane laughed and said, "Whut'd you say? Did you hear what you said? You said 'county.' Honey, we don't have any counties in this state, they're parishes, or have you forgotten that? Boy, you've been in Texas too long."

She's right you know. At last count, I have been gone from Louisiana for 29 years. I guess that's long enough to forget that it is the only state in the union with parishes.

A friend of mine from Louisiana asked me the other day: "You've been living in Texas for a long time, do you consider yourself a Texan?" That answer took some thought. It was like asking me which of my recently-divorced parents I cared about the most.

Being in sales, I tend to use my dual-citizenship to my advantage. If customers want to talk about Texas, I'm Big Tex. They think we all live on a big horse ranch anyway with an oil well in the back yard, wear a Stetson, and have a six-gun strapped to our legs.

I've learned that very few outsiders have any concept of how large Texas is. When I worked for a Seattle company, they called us once to ask if the hurricane they read about hitting Houston had any effect on us in Dallas. I said, yeah boy, it hit Houston and came right up the coast of Dallas. They said, "Yep, that's what we figured."

The hardest time I have being a Texan is when I'm around a group of native Californians. They don't cotton to Texans much. They always want to talk about our gun laws, the death penalty and our environmental record.

Years ago I ran into a couple of the Sequoia huggers at a black jack table in Vegas. I knew right away I was in for trouble. I was outnumbered and my six guns were up in my hotel room.

They started our verbal duel like this:

SH: You're from the South right, which part?"
Me: Texas, partner. Where you boys out of?

SH: California, the Bay Area. So you're from Texas, huh? You guys have the death penalty over there, right? Anybody complain much about that?

Me: Just the ones we aim to kill

SH: Texas is primarily a Republican state right? So, you probably don't care much for President Clinton?

Me: No, on the contrary. We invite him down to Dallas every November for a parade, but he won't come.

SH: I'm sure you are aware that Texas has a horrible record on the environment. Care to make any comment about that, Tex?

Me: Just one. Save the whales!

SH: Well? Now, that's encouraging…

Me: Yep, we'll eat them last...

Even though I live in Texas now, I like to think I have the muddy water of my home state still flowing through my veins. I'll leave you with these words I wrote some years ago. It's called Louisiana Time.

Big snake hanging from a willow tree
Gator floating by a cypress knee
Each one doing just what he please
Living in Louisiana time

Pirogue cuts just like a knife
Through the water that's a Cajun's life
Dark and brown like dirty rice
Simmering in Louisiana time

The Fleur-de-lis she's calling me
Through fog so thick that I can't see
I'm going back to where I'm supposed to be
Back in Louisiana time

Louisiana's got a way of keeping
Time where it needs to be
Flowing so soft and smooth
Like a river to the sea

Down here we got a passion
For the cypress and the pine
And in every heart there's beating

A little Louisiana time

Geauxing Crazy

It's early August and I can't wait for football season to get here. For me, having to watch TV golf and baseball in June and July is the equivalent of Kane from Kung Fu walking a year alone in the desert.

Tonight I'm held up in the penthouse of the Super 8 in Ruston and watching a replay of a 2006 game between LSU and Alabama. Boy does this bring back memories.

Growing up, I was an avid LSU football fan - as was my father. He would actually make the three and one half hour drive to Baton Rouge on game day, attend the game, then drive back that night with Mama asleep on the back seat.

The first LSU game I remember watching on TV was the 1966 Cotton Bowl victory against The University of Arkansas. I was ten at the time.

LSU had a 5' 9" running back named Joe Labruzzo. The *Dallas Morning News* later described him a dwarfish tailback. He was so small he just sort of got lost in the midst of his large linemen until he finally appeared in the end zone.

Big games like that we could get on the TV. Most of the games we could only get over the radio. Daddy would have the Tiger game dialed in on Saturday night and sit up in his bed until it was over. We listened together the night Ruston's own Bert Jones, with no time left on the clock, tossed a pass to tailback Brad Davis to beat Ole Miss.

Of course the Rebel fans claimed the clock had run out before the snap. They even hung a banner as you entered Mississippi from Louisiana that read, "Welcome to Mississippi, please set your clock ahead 3 seconds."

Later in 1971, we were part of a national TV audience that watched Bert and his Bengal Tiger team beat Ara Parsegian's Notre Dame team 28-8 in Baton

Rouge. That night the LSU fans tore down the goal posts in Tiger Stadium. I think that was the day my blood officially went from being red to purple and gold.

LSU football has a rich history. There's the 1959 Billy Cannon Halloween night run when he broke a bunch of tackles in a touchdown run to help beat arch rival Ole Miss. Back when we played them every year, they would replay that run over TV and the radio. The man who made the historic call of the run on the radio was J.C. Politz, and coincidentally, he was my retired neighbor during my second year in Baton Rouge.

I don't know for sure it the story is true or not, but I heard that my cousin Sid Colvin was in attendance but didn't see the run because an overly excited and well-oiled Tiger fan knocked him down some bleachers.

I probably shouldn't tell this story on myself, but I will. Growing up in a dry parish and in a somewhat sheltered environment, I hadn't had much experience with alcohol. I had never participated in any pre-game activities either. Now it was time to attend my very first LSU football game as a freshman.

Harry Hawks grew up in New Orleans. He was a real nice guy who lived in my apartment complex. He asked me what I was doing for the first home game. I said, I don't know, why?

He said, well we all get together at my apartment before the game, eat and drink, then we all walk over to Tiger stadium around 5:30 when the gates go up so we can get some really good seats. You want to join us?

Since I was new to town, it sounded like a good plan to me, so I said sure.

When I got to Harry's apartment the conversation went something like this:

Harry: Hey Randy! What you want to drink?

Me: Oh, I don't know. What you got?

Harry: We got beer, vodka, gin, scotch and bourbon.

Me: Hmm. Got anything that doesn't taste too much like alcohol?

Harry: Sure. That's bourbon and Coke. I'll fix you one. A couple of the girls will stick a flask in their purse so we can have some more while we're at the game.

It was the 1974 season and, according to the Chinese calendar, the Year of the Tiger with talk of being a potential national champion. We were kicking the season off against the Colorado Buffalos. LSU creamed them, or so I was told.

I got creamed early by the bourbon and Coke. So creamed I couldn't even stand for the National Anthem. Harry and a buddy had to carry me out of the stadium like firemen removing a victim of smoke inhalation from a burning building.

Since then, I've learned how to behave myself during LSU ballgames, although my kids would tell you how they used to hide my TV remote because they saw me throw it at our Curtis Mathis one fall afternoon after the Tigers blew a late game lead. My passion for LSU football runs just as deep today.

It's like that story about a ball boy who went to fetch an out of bounds punt during a sold out LSU home game. He noticed a very rare empty seat next to an elderly woman.

He asked the lady, Ma'am, why is it that you have an empty seat? She said that's where my late husband used to sit. The ball boy asked, Ma'am, why didn't you give the ticket to one of your relatives? She said, I would have, but they're all at the funeral.

Hah! Geaux Tigers!

The Angel Took the Bus

It's late August 2007. It's been two years since Hurricane Katrina did its best to wash away the collective soul of my native state of Louisiana; months since the levees were repaired and Lake Ponchartrain was refilled with our tears.

I know that it's going to take years, if not decades, to repair the damage left in the wake of that storm. It may take more time than that to regain the trust of those federal and state institutions we send our tax dollars to and hope for something in return.

It brought back bad memories the other night to watch Spike Lee's four part saga, When the Levees Broke, on HBO. One by one the folks interviewed told their stories of thinking they might die waiting for a crummy bottle of water and the country that, as President John F. Kennedy once put it, "could land a man on the moon and return him safely to Earth," couldn't find a way to get it to them.

North to south, Louisiana is a proud state made up of proud people. I said Amen when I heard one displaced New Orleans resident respond to a TV reporter's question, "How does it feel to be a refugee?" He snapped back, "I ain't no damned refugee. I'm an American!"

Danged right he's an American, I thought, and I'll bet, by the grace of God,. he was born a Southerner too. Leave him alone, you big New York TV station Connie Chung-looking outfit!

One of the other interviewees in Lee's piece pointed out that if Louisiana had the opportunity to keep its oil and gas revenues, it would be as rich as Saudi Arabia. Then, he said, we wouldn't need any help. We'd just take this opportunity to remodel our homes, repave our streets in gold, and be happy once again.

One story coming out of Katrina I'll always remember is about this guy named Jabbar Gibson who, after being told that no one could get in or out of the evacuation area, showed up out of nowhere with a school bus. He loaded up all the evacuees the bus would hold and headed for the Houston Astrodome.

Jabbar had been in a little trouble before with the law and he's had some trouble since, but that simple and incredible act of heroism that day by a 20-year old New Orleans resident saved lives and inspired me to write a poem about him.

It's called "Angel in the School Bus."

Hurricane Katrina
That lady sho was mean
She dumped a lot of water
On the town of New Orleans

We waded up to our necks
Tried to get to higher ground
Nobody there to help us
Lots of bodies floating 'round

Had no food or water
Knew the end was near
When a man drove up in a school bus
Said, "I'm gonna get ya'll out of here"

We pitched in all our money
Bought some gas and we were gone
With the angel in the school bus
We were headed to the Astrodome

Somebody said he stole it
Some said that it was wrong
That the angel in a school bus
Got us to the Astrodome

Man in Houston stopped us at the gate
Said sorry, you don't belong
Took one look at our angel's face
And said ya'll welcome to the Astrodome

I wanted to shake his hand
I turned but he was gone
Who was that sweet angel?
He got us to the Astrodome

Whenever I felt like it was good sport to make light of somebody about their circumstances, for being too homely, too short, or something along those lines,

Mama would say: "Now Randy, that person didn't ask for that. That's God's doing.

They didn't have a choice in the matter. Don't you think, if they had, they would have done something about it? It could just as easily been you. Would you want somebody teasing you for something you couldn't help, something you couldn't do anything about?"

Mama could have used a curling iron on me and not gotten a lesson to stick to my soul any better.

Growing up fairly poor herself, she always had compassion for the underdog. Two years ago, the people of the Gulf Coast and New Orleans became overnight underdogs. She would have done all she could to help them.

Whether or not you consider Hurricane Katrina to be of God's doing, the aftermath was something those people didn't ask for and now must learn to live with.

It's like the man said, they ain't no damned refugees, they're Americans, just like me and you.

And on the second anniversary of this disaster, let's not forget that.

Chapter Three

With All Due Respect

And Miles to Go

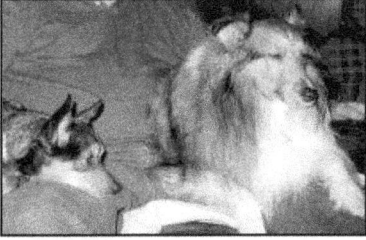

My oldest son Brian Rogers named our Sheltie after the jazz great Miles Davis.

It's an odd name for a dog I know, but considering he named our other dog, a Chihuahua mix, Tatiana, because he thought she looked Russian, I guess that name makes just as much sense.

Brian brought the little Russian-Mexican doggie princess home as a replacement for our cat Ebony who passed away in 2006. He said we needed another female presence in the home to keep Miles honest and to torment him accordingly.

Bless her heart, Tatiana's been a great little addition to the family, but she can be a little overly sensitive at times. For example, whenever she gives me a reason to scold her, she gets down on her stomach and belly crawls under the couch. I think she does that just to make me laugh.

The modern age of Rogers' pet ownership all started years ago when my wife was researching a good dog to get the kids. She showed me this book she had with a picture of a breed that looked a lot like a miniature Lassie.

The book said this Shetland sheepdog breed, the Sheltie, was smart, loyal, and good with kids. I asked her why I didn't have a book like that when we were dating. Her page would have said smart, loyal, and would be best married to a rich dentist, jeweler, or antique collector.

Miles is the second Sheltie we've had. The first one was named Jack. I think Brian named him after one of the presidents, maybe Eisenhower. Now that he has gone on up to doggie heaven, I can say this without hurting his feelings that he wasn't near as smart as Miles. Jack was real hyper too, ran around in circles all the time, and barked a lot.

So much so that one day I said we should write the publisher of that breed book and suggest they add this line to the Sheltie description: smart, loyal, great with kids, runs in circles, and barks at atoms.

I guess they don't have harmonicas on the Shetland Islands because Miles can't stand the sound of my playing "Love Me Do" on mine. He looks constipated and howls like he's got a cactus thorn in his paw.

I find that strange too because Shetland is part of Scotland, a place well known for its bagpipe playing. How can a dog breed whose ancestors listened to that noise for centuries find a harmonica that revolting?

He finds it so distasteful he once even nipped me on the heel to get me to stop. It's the same thing they do when they want sheep in the field to change direction. Just to see if it was a matter of song preference, I tried playing "Oh Shenandoah" but no, he started a low growl and gnarled his teeth at me to indicate that he'd just as soon I stop playing all together.

Miles is by far the smartest dog I've ever had. He sleeps on his back like a human, understands conversational English, and will follow most hand signals. He's even amber dogsterous and can shake your hand with either paw.

I can say, "Let's go get the mail," and he'll run to the front door and wait for me to open it. The day I taught him to do that I couldn't wait for the kids to get home from school so I could show him off.

I said, "Watch this; you won't believe what I taught Miles to do." I said, "Miles, let's go get the mail." He just sat there and looked at me like I was speaking Latin, or some other language in which he was not quite as conversational.

I asked him what was wrong, "Why aren't you showing the kids our new trick?"

He said, "Mail doesn't run at 5 p.m. Besides, we already went and got it, remember?"

See? I told you that dog was smart.

Don't Tell 'At

Friends at Campbell's One Stop
"The Coffee Shop in Dubach, La."

I was in Ruston this past weekend enjoying another fine stay in the plush penthouse suite of the Super 8. I didn't sleep very well this time.

I think it might have had something to do with the motel pillows. They were as hard as something Moses might have carried down the mountain.

Now don't get me wrong, I'm not saying the motel isn't comfortable, it is. It could only be better if I was out by the pool being fed peeled grapes by native, but since they put the winter cover over the pool, it just wouldn't look right.

My room almost came with a sunken bath though. A few more showers with the curtain on the outside should finish that project.

Although I ordered a single room, I did have two well-behaved roaches show up to share my sleeping quarters. Mama wouldn't want me sharing this fact, but I grew up with roaches.

Unless I unexpectedly find them in my house shoes, they don't bother me at all. In fact, I'll go as far as to say that I consider North Louisiana roaches to be world-class. You can't beat them for their size, speed, and agility.

And once you get to know them, their conversational skills can be well above average.

Before I checked out, I overheard two of them debating whether they should take what was left of my Quiznos sandwich and eat it there or take it with them. I told them not to hurry on my account.

I enjoy going back home now more than ever. If for nothing else, I get to pick up some new material for my newspaper column. Lord knows it's a target-rich environment whenever I show up in the morning at the Campbell's One Stop, the coffee shop on the hill in Dubach. The coffee will cost you, but the stories are free.

Like my roach friends, but for different reasons, I consider the Dubach story tellers to be world-class as well. The king of the coffee shop humor circuit, Bill Pendergrass, missed his calling. He could make a living at any stand up comedy house in America. In fact, he's so good at story telling, that when I've finished my coffee and I'm ready to leave, I'm looking around for a tip jar.

Bill graciously yields the table to some other story telling side-splitters like James Fuller, Seth Tatum, Richard "Dicky" Lewis and Billy Don Knowles, all plenty capable in their own right.

I can't remember when I've laughed so much or so hard. Some stories start off with, "Well, you remember old so and so? Well, here's something I bet you didn't know about him…"

I think the next time I'll visit the coffee shop armed with a tape recorder and plenty of batteries. That way I won't miss anything. While I'll do my best to get most of the stories down, you can bet that some of them won't be suitable for outside consumption.

Just like Vegas, most of the time we loyal listeners will abide by the what's-told-at-the-coffee-shop-stays-at-the coffee-shop rule. Repeating a story out of school might cause one to get banned and subsequently lose the opportunity for Himalayan-like wisdom and enlightenment.

It's just like when I was a kid sitting at the dinner table and heard something I wasn't supposed to hear, much less repeat, a family member would always say, "Now Randy, don't tell that!" Only, in typical Southern fashion, it always came out sounding like one word: Nowdontellat!

You can think of it like the FBI warning on a rented DVD? You know, before the movie starts, when it says something about how the redistribution of this content is strictly prohibited?

Well, that's just the FBI's way of saying Nowdontellat!

Breakfast with the Angels

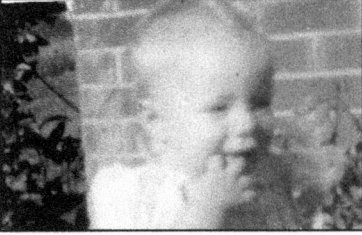

Laura Ann Rogers

Did you ever see the scene from the movie *The Sixth Sense* when little Haley Joel Osment tells Bruce Willis, "I see dead people?" That film represented the freaky notion that the young boy could see

and talk to those who have passed on. As far fetched as that idea is, I think it might be interesting to have a paranormal parley with some of the dearly departed.

Unless they make house calls, my conversation would have to take place at the Hamilton Cemetery in Dubach where most of my immediate family is interred.

It might go something like this:

Me: Hey PawPaw

PawPaw: That my little padnah?!

Me: Yes. Well, I'm fifty now PawPaw and I'm not that little anymore.

PawPaw: Yeah, I noticed. When you walked up you blocked out the sun. Could you step back a few? You're tilting my casket.

Me: Oh real funny. Is Mama around?

Mama: I'm here baby. I've been keeping an eye on you. Lewis Grizzard tells me that you're writing for some sort of newspaper? He said you couldn't carry his typewriter, but I don't pay him any mind.

Now tell your mother, are you making good money writing your little columns?

Me: Well, sorta, I uh…It's a gorgeous day out, wouldn't you say Mama? I love these crisp fall mornings. The leaves are just beginning to turn and…

Larnell: Uh huh, I thought so. Don't you dare leave your day job! You're still a mess.

Me: Yes Ma'am. I get it honest, I guess. Is Granny around?

Granny: Hello, young sprig! I can't talk long, my piece is about to come on.

Me: You still watching *As the World Turns* up here? I don't want to make you miss it.

Granny: Don't worry, I've got it TiVoed. You want to speak to your sisters? I think they have some questions for you…girls?

Joan: Me first. Did you really fill Daddy's Buick's gas tank up with water?

Me: Huh? Why? Where'd you hear that? Well yes, back when there was such a person, I think I was pretending to be a gas station attendant.

Laura Ann: Okay my turn. Did you really try to flush your pet beagle, Lucky Doodle, down the commode just because you were tired of feeding him?

Me: Aw come on…did Mama put ya'll up to this? Mama?? Where's St. Peter? I need to lodge a complaint.

Okay, let's get back down to Earth a bit as they say. Probably for some good reason, some things like this are not meant to be. While I had many good years with my grandmother, grandfather, and mother, I never got to know my sister Joan (pronounced Jo Ann).

Like me, she was born premature. Back then the hospital in Ruston didn't have incubators and she passed away in a closet there after only 5 days. My big sister Jean was only 2 at the time so she can't tell me much about her. It would have been nice to get to know Joan a little.

The same goes for Laura Ann. She was only two when she died. I was 6 at the time so I can't remember that much about her, but I still have fond memories of what it was like to be her big brother.

My memory of the others is still as clear as a bell. Like the names they had for me: When PawPaw would be out and about with me under foot, his men friends would ask him, "Doc, who you got there with you?" He'd always say, "That's my little padnah!"

For some reason, Granny always referred to me as "young sprig." The dictionary says that's a young, immature person. When she was calling me that, I was.

When Mama was a nurse and would see me coming down the hall to see her at the Green Clinic she would always embarrass me by yelling out, "There's my Babeeee!!"

So I hope you'll indulge me this once for wishing that I could talk to them again. To me, that's just not quite as weird as it sounds.

Mama Knew Best

It's easy now to say that she was the number one influence in my life, a little harder to say that I didn't always listen to her sage advice.

Growing up, I know at times it looked like I wasn't paying attention, but I heard every word she said. The sound of her voice is just as clear to me today as it was back then.

One day I was sitting at the kitchen table, doing my homework. She was washing dishes. I asked her what the hardest substance known to man was.

She said, "Dried egg."

Whenever I started a question with "Mama?" her response was always, "Whababy?" When she wasn't calling me Baby, it was Randall. Nobody ever called me Randall but her. When she wanted to make sure I heard what she was saying, she called me David Randall, usually with the word *now* in front of it. "Now, David Randall, you better listen to me."

Whenever she shouted "David Randall Rogers!," I knew to take off running and not look back to find out what I did to get in that much trouble. All three names meant it was something big.

When my oldest son Brian was a little boy, he once called me Sweebaby. I asked him where he got that from.

He said, "That's what Nanny says when I ask her a question. She says, Whut, sweebaby?"

Whababy and Sweebaby, now there's a lady who knew how to talk to little boys like me and Brian.

Laura Nell Rogers loved having the "the girls" over for a bridge party. They had a local club and I guess, at one time or the other, every lady in town sat at a folding bridge table in our house.

When I rode my bike up and there were a dozen cars at our house I knew that it was either bridge night or that she had finally shot Daddy. How relieved I was when I got close enough to hear the ladies laughing. Nobody could find a husband shootin' *that* funny.

I learned a lot sitting at Mama's kitchen table. Like one day when she said, "You know, whenever somebody asks you how you're doing, it's better to just say 'fine thanks.' That's because they really don't want to know how you're doing. Not really. Most of the time, they're just being nice, making conversation. Tell them you're fine and you'll keep your friends around a lot longer."

Well, like I said, I was listening to her but I thought her theories should be tested from time to time so the next person that asked me how I was doing I said some really bizarre like: "Well, I've got just a touch of blood in my urine, but other than that, I'm doing just fine." I knew she was right when I saw their eyes glaze over.

I'll leave you with a piece of a song I wrote about Mama. It has references to my early memories of the Colvin Family Reunion, a photo I once saw of my great aunt Laura in her garden wearing a bonnet, and a tribute to Mama's favorite hymn - Amazing Grace. It's called *Mama Sang.*

At those family reunions
Where I was made to go
Uncle Frank brought the famous bread
He made from sour dough
The men folk pitched their horseshoes
The lemonade was cold
And I was much too young to see
My Mama getting old

She sat there in her bonnet
With all the lines of age
Read to me from the book of life
And then turned another page

Mama Sang Amazing Grace
Until the day she died
I can taste her Sunday dinner
And the chicken that she fried

On the day my Mama passed
I heard the church bells ring
Every time I hear them now
I can hear my mama sing

Amazing grace, how sweet the sound…

The Wizard of Op

As Archie Bunker used to put it, my principal fought in "WWII, the big one."

The big one for him was the Battle of the Bulge. It was Germany's huge counteroffensive in Belgium that came dangerously close to turning the war back around in the enemy's favor.

He served in the U.S. Tank Corps under General George S. Patton, Jr. Maybe that's where he got his toughness.

After the war, he returned to my hometown to become a deacon in our church, a science teacher, football coach, and later the first school principal I ever knew who wasn't a Colvin.

Before him was M.O. "Cricket" Colvin and after him was Mr. Doug "Coach" Colvin. At our school, Colvins normally ascended to the principal's chair the way the Windsors ascend to the British throne.

The first time I remember getting sent to his office for corrective action, the recommended punishment was that I stay after school that day and pick up trash along the school grounds.

It worked out well because I had to stay for the 3:30 bus anyway. Since I lived on the outskirts of town, Ms. Avis Campbell had to make her in-town run and then come back and get me and the real country kids at 3:30.

I was the designated bus crier. It was quite an honor. While the other kids were seeing how high they could get the swings to go before they jumped off or were tossing washers, I stood watch for the school bus.

Like Ahab in *Moby Dick*, at first sight of the great yellow bus rounding the corner, I would yell as loud as I could, "BUUUUSSSSSSSSS!!!!!!!!!" That way everybody had plenty of time to get their books together before Ms. Avis got there.

72

With my trusted delegate handling my bus crier duties for that day, I met my principal outside his office and we walked together picking up candy wrappers and empty Coke bottles.

When we were done, he said, "Okay," and then he handed me a nickel and told me to go get me a Coke.

That's the way I'll always remember him – tough, but always with a sweet side he saved for school kids, like me, who really wanted to do right.

I think it was Mike Davis who gave him the nickname Op because whenever he said "Uh," it sounded more like "Op." Of course, nobody ever said op or anything else like that to his face unless they had a death wish.

He was freaky strong. Once when a high school kid was making trouble we saw him pick the kid up off the floor with one arm and take him to the office.

He was one of those people who didn't have to raise his voice to get your attention.

He also served as our principal at the time we were going through school integration. Those were tough and tense times.

One day Larry Crawford used the spring in his ink pen to propel it so that it stuck into the drop-down ceiling in the Ms. Wesley's class room.

She was the pretty new black teacher who came over from the all-black Hopewell schools to teach math.

Larry refused her orders to get up and retrieve the pen so she went to get the principal. Of course he promptly retrieved the pen when the principal asked him to.

As was often his habit, he used the pen to clean his ears as he delivered his lecture about what all he wouldn't tolerate from any school kid.

His favorite line was, "I don't care if your name is Billy, Bobby, Suzy, Mary, or Johnny. You won't act like that in this school."

With the traditional respect and reverence he commanded, not a word was said, much less laughter heard, when he turned to leave and blue ink was seen running down from his ear.

When his son Vance Lewis was killed in a car wreck near Cyprus bottom, it hit him and his family hard. It hit the whole town hard.

Vance had been a multi-sport star athlete. So many ball teams came from all over North Louisiana to pay their respects at the funeral that they had to stand outside on the steps of the First Baptist Church.

I don't think Mr. Lewis was ever the same after that.

I understand the amphitheater (shown above) that now stands on the southwest bank of James Lake in Dubach was built in his memory. What a fitting tribute it is to such a tough and sweet man and one that I'll never forget.

Mr. Elwood "Dick" Lewis, my principal, may he rest in peace.

Through These Eyes

I had the best time recently going back to the first annual Dubach Baptist Church reunion. Founded in 1901, you'd think we'd had one by now but nevertheless it was just the way I remembered it before I pointed my 1969 Buick GS 400 south towards LSU and left town for good in 1974.

Before the sermon, Jo Tatum walked over and handed the portable microphone to Mr. Floyd Mercer who spoke movingly about how his family first came to Dubach from Texas knowing nary a soul and how the church opened its arms and heart and made them feel welcome.

Then my cousin, the ageless Gill Colvin, came to the podium to speak touchingly about the good days and good people gone by and how nobody could deliver the church report like the late Eugene Hamilton.

During the sermon, I fidgeted in my seat the same way I did 33 years ago. It's something about those pew cushions and my posterior that don't get along. It could have also been because I didn't have Stevie Carrico or Terry Dick and a good game of hangman going to take my mind off of my discomfort.

After the services, we all filed into the large church fellowship hall where there was a half-mile long table of every kind of dish imaginable.

With the full understanding that none of the food came courtesy of NutriSystem or delivered the Glycemic Advantage^T, my plate soon runneth over and I took my seat at a table next to Larry Bilberry.
Larry started the conversation off by saying, "I bet you don't recognize me." But I did, and I said so.

It's funny, I was the one most people didn't recognize. I'm sure that leaving town at 18 and 165 pounds and coming back at 51 and, shall we say, a little more filled out contributes to that.

Larry and his family lived on our block next door to Tommy and Glenn Miller and were famous for hosting homemade ice-cream yard parties. That's where I learned how to add ice, rock salt, and take my turn at the crank if I wanted a bowl of vanilla or peach ice cream.

After I was married and had kids, we bought an ice cream maker that had a motor you plugged in that spun the cylinder in the ice and rock salt. Consequently my young kids never got their turn at the crank.

Back to the reunion, I was struck by how pretty the women of the church still were. The likes of Baby Trammell, Mary Gray, Jo Tatum, Fern Newsom, Sarah and Betty Colvin, and all the others have of course gotten older but they have certainly not lost their stylish beauty, elegance, Southern charm and grace.

I wrote a song years ago about a fine Southern lady who once told me that, while her wrinkles meant that she was growing old on the outside, from the inside looking out, she still had the eyes of a little girl.

It was a beautiful notion that I'll always remember. Here's some of what I wrote. It's called "Through These Eyes"

She sat in her old rocking' chair
And I brushed her hair
The way I always do
We talked a lot about getting old
And I wanted to know
How it changes you. She said …

Through these eyes, I'm still a little girl
And I still see the world
The way I always have
Through these eyes there's no getting old
Long as my little girl's soul
Still sees the world
Through these eyes

I'll never doubt the role my church and its fellowship played in my life. Going back this time meant a lot to me. I hope to go again next year. It will be that one day a year when I feel like I'm back where I belong.

To Die For

M.J. was quite a character with his bad right foot and the stubbed cigar that was always hanging from his mouth, old. He lived across the street from us in the early '80's when we lived in Texarkana, TX.

Back when people didn't pump their own gas, he owned a full-service station on Texas Boulevard.

This is going to sound a little silly, but M.J. was so good to us that I remember one time my car running out of gas right as I got to his station. After passing up numerous opportunities to get gas, I coasted into his station. I don't know about you, but whether it's a barber, butcher, or a candlestick maker; once I develop a good relationship with a vendor, I'm loyal for life. To me, stopping at another station would be the equivalent of cheating on my spouse. That loyalty to M.J. almost had me walking to his station with a gas can in my hand and probably passing a few stations along the way.

One day I was chatting with another neighbor, David Johnson, when M. J.'s name came up.

"You *do* know who M.J. is don't you," David asked.

Sure, he's my neighbor and runs a gas station, why?

"Oh, more than that," David went on. "Remember the 1966 University of Texas tower shooting down in Austin? M.J. and his family were headed up to the observation deck of the tower when they surprised the sniper. Four of them were shot, two died, his sister Marguerite and his son Mark. His wife Mary and his other son Mike were shot but survived. Sometimes you'll see Mike sitting in the service station behind the counter.

"When the Austin police got up to where M.J. was, M.J. came out with a bloody pair of white women's shoes and said to officer Martinez of the Austin Police, 'Let me have your gun, he killed my whole family.' They said they had to wrestle with M.J. to restrain him. He would've killed the sniper, Charles Whitman, that day given a gun and the chance or he would have surely died trying. That's our neighbor – M.J. Gabour You really never heard that story?"

I'm reminded of this story because of what happened recently in Blacksburg, VA with another gunman at another college who killed 33 students and faculty at Virginia Tech. Before that, it was the shootings at Columbine and the little Amish school in Pennsylvania.

In 1999 I wrote a poem that was published in a book put together by Sue Goode of Littleton, CO titled "Columbine, We Will Remember." I'd like to share it with you. The title of the poem was "Sad Times at Columbine - When They Kill Our Children."

When they kill our children, our hearts and minds implode
Our lives are filled with loneliness and we bear a heavy load
When they kill our children, we stay awake at night
If sleep comes, it's deep with sweat with images of their fright

When they kill our children, we ask each other why
Ask those questions of our Maker and sing of the sweet by and by
When they kill our children, they've taken all our best
Taken the future from our lives and laid them all to rest

When they kill our children, I'm ashamed to hate them all
For it makes me a lesser person and as a Christian I feel small
When they kill our children, the acorn will never be a tree
A forest without rejuvenation is what it means to me

I'm not sure what a chance knowing of my neighbor M.J. Gabour or having a poem published in a book of remembrance of Columbine have in common or might mean in the grand scheme of things.

I do know that a little piece of humanity dies every time we see our youngest laid to waste. In the sense that they are our most innocent, our most precious, it is the ultimate in sin for someone to take the acorns of our oaks and see that they never grow to their maturity.

That's why my neighbor M.J. Gabour wanted that gun.

Just like the professor at Virginia Tech who died holding the door shut so his students could get out a window and away from a gunman, to not do so would mean the loss of life of many more innocents.

Isn't that one of the things worth dying for?

I hope that if ever I could summon the courage to do it, it would be for me.

Our First Angels

If you were traveling through downtown Dubach headed in the direction of the old cotton gin, you passed the Butler's home on your left. The building next to their home with the almost-always-open door was the cleaners they owned and operated.

They had to leave the door open during the day to let the heat out from the dryers and the presses.

If you could stand shopping in the heat, they also sold clothes in there. Back in the 60's, that's where I could go buy a pair of white double-knit bell-bottomed pants, a wide leather belt, or a god-awful loud shirt with a collar so wide it could choke me during a strong wind.

Whenever Mama went to the post office, I would take that opportunity to scoot across the street to the cleaners and the red soft drink machine that sat on their front stoop.

It was the kind you put your money in then open up a door to pull the drink out. I would sit cross-legged in the green and white metal lawn chair, sip my cold Coke, and watch for Mama to come out of the post office.

They had a metal bottle rack mounted on the wall and every kid in town knew to place their empties there when they were finished. I guess when you grow up in a small town with very few locked doors; kids just sorta learn to adopt the honor system.

I was more concerned that Mama wouldn't give me enough time to finish my drink and that I'd have to place a half-full bottle in the rack before rejoining her.

Ms. Monette was the matriarch of the Butler family and one of my mother's best friends. She was a member of the card-playing, coffee-drinking coterie that Mama referred to simply and collectively as "the girls."

On Saturday mornings, Mama and Ms. Monette Butler would sit and drink coffee while their youngest son Tony and I watched cartoons.

During my high school days, their oldest son, Jimmy, gave me a weekend job at their washateria across the street from Tech. I was in charge of making change for the washers and dryers, sweeping the floors, and making sure no one made off with the small black and white television I watched most of the time.

Martha Lou was their middle child. She was a couple of years older than me. I hadn't seen her since high school. Harvey Davis called me one day to tell me that she was very sick and that she had called and asked him to be on of her pallbearers. I've never heard of someone doing that. It must have taken a great deal of inner strength.

The newspaper said she went to Tech to become a nurse and that one of her passions was caring for the elderly at Alpine Nursing Home. In that role, I imagine that she helped many of their residents depart our world.

I'm reminded of a verse from an old Blood, Sweat & Tears song:

I'm not scared of dying
And I don't really care
If it's peace you find in dying
Then let the time be near

When the time is near, I believe Martha Lou, and others who work with the elderly, the sick and the dying, are the very first angels we see.

With a soft voice and the warm touch of a hand, these first angels help prepare us for our walk through the valley of the shadow of death. They help us to find peace in dying.

Martha Lou Butler Gallemore left us on April 10, 2008 to be with the other angels. May she rest in peace.

People Get Ready

Being raised in a small town had its advantages. Everything in town was just a bike ride away. Doors were rarely locked. I had two drug stores to choose from each with a soda fountain where I could get a chocolate malt for just a quarter and one that even allowed me to read the latest Mad magazine for free. I'm sure that's where I first learned that Alfred E. Newman and I shared the same what-me-worry outlook on life.

Across the street we had two hardware stores. Henry and Company was where Mama took me each year to get a new pair of Keds or Converse tenny shoes. While Mama was still inside paying for them, I'd run up and down the sidewalks of Dubach to make sure they could pass the speed test. I could never run faster than on the first day I got my new sneaks.

Buster Delony's dairy, manure, and mosquito farm was only a block away from my house. It had a big hay barn where I could play hide-and seek-with my friends from the neighborhood.

A pen was adjacent to the dairy and home to a gray-humped Brahma bull. My little Daisy BB gun with the plastic stock couldn't break a window, but it sure could make a bull mad if I hit him in a certain place. I don't think Mr. Buster ever caught on to why his prized bull might not have been in the mood some days.

I loved growing up in a small town, but to be fair, sometime it had its disadvantages. For one, the vast snitch network that existed there could get word of my misdeeds home faster than I could prepare a plausible cover story. It's been said about a small town that the only way to keep people from knowing about something is not to do it.

Grammy winning singer-songwriter John Cougar Mellencamp grew up in Seymour, Indiana, a town just a little smaller than Ruston. He wrote some nice words about his home town:

> I was born in a small town
> Educated in a small town
> Taught to feel Jesus in a small town

Used to daydream in that small town
Another boring romantic that's me
No I cannot forget where it is that I come from
I cannot forget the people who love me
Yeah, I can be myself here in this small town
And people let me be just what I want to be

Not too long ago, I had the opportunity to go back and speak to the kids from my old high school. They all assembled in the cafeteria to hear me talk about my best selling book* *The Pine Cone Collection* and about reading and writing in general.

I got a wonderful reception from the kids. Although when I asked them how many were there just to get out of class, I think the show of hands was unanimous. That's okay. You could have rolled in a cold cadaver when I was a student there if it got me out of Algebra II.

While I was there I talked about how small town kids are special and how we're different from big city kids. For one, we're not ducking drive-bys to go to school. I wanted them to know that I believe growing up in a small town gives you an advantage. It means you're naturally more friendly and people-oriented than other kids. You have to be.

And some of these kids can really write! They showed me some great work during a writing roundtable. With John and Susan Hays' blessing, hopefully we can soon showcase some of their talents in T*he Morning Paper.*

Then you'll be able to see what small town kids can do when they put their minds to it and are given the opportunity! So ya'll get ready!

*in Dubach

Somewhere in the Ballpark

I was having lunch the other day with my childhood-friend-turned-billionaire, Tycoon Pendergrass, when the subject of the baseball park in Dubach came up.

"You *do* you realize that we had one the finest baseball parks in the state of Louisiana," Ty said. "It was one of the only high school parks at the time with lights in the outfield, a manned scoreboard, and a press box."

He's right, you know, and I hadn't thought of that park in years.

Before Coach Doug Colvin, I can't remember who saw to it that parcel of land was a source of community pride. I know that Coach Billy Henderson succeeded Coach Colvin and not a single blade of grass suffered for it.

When you played baseball for either, an additional position was that of grounds keeper. After each game or practice, we had to "drag the field" which meant being draft horses behind this wooden frame with spikes on the underside and pull it along the infield. Outfielders and pitchers usually did that while the infielders hand-raked their position.

I practically grew up in that ballpark. I guess it all started age five or six when I played Peewee baseball. I still remember the day my friend-since-the-first-grade-but-not-a-billionaire-yet Ronnie Smith told me they were starting a league and that I needed to choose what position I wanted to play.

There was one small problem: I didn't know that baseball had positions. Heck, I'm not even sure that I knew the bases were numbered. But as a child, I can now openly stipulate that I was somewhat sheltered and as a result tended to be a tad on the dumb side.

Since then, my stupidity has grown to a new level. In fact, you could fill the Caspian Sea with the things I don't know. Like just the other day, I asked a pretty stupid question of a friend of mine, someone I consider to be a fairly bright fellow. He stared at me for a minute, and then remarked, "Man, you are sucking all the dumb out of the room."

Now you would think that statement would hurt my feelings, but no. In fact, I'm proud to finally be getting the respect I so richly deserve. You can't get to my level of stupidity overnight. Now, back to the ball park.

Whether or not we had any talent for baseball or even knew the bases were numbered, nearly every kid in town signed up that year to play baseball. And I think there was a rule in the book somewhere to that every kid had to play at least a full inning.

Probably shortly after I asked my coach why the outfield positions weren't also numbered, he put me in right field. That's where they put players of my caliber so we don't cause too much damage.

At that age, playing right field is downright boring. I was so far away from the action they were kind enough to help me by yelling "RANDY? BALL!" whenever something concerning baseball was headed my way.

That wake up call was quite necessary too because I might be sitting down, tossing my glove up in the air, or just staring off into space.

Like me, Stephen Norris was exiled to right field one day when a ground ball was hit out to him. He went to chase after the ball and slipped down. We were all laughing when we heard him yell "Snake!"

I'll bet you a Ken Griffey, Jr. baseball card that Stephen Norris was the only kid in history to have a water moccasin contribute to an inside-the-park home run. Makes you wonder how they would have scored that.

Another memorable right field occurrence involved William Fuller. Nothing as interesting as slipping on snake mind you, but during one game he was chasing after a ball when his cap blew off.

Instead of continuing to run bareheaded, he went back and retrieved his cap, put it back on, straightened it, then went on to get the ball. Meanwhile the batter is rounding the bases.

Later back in the dugout, we could only nod in agreement when William gave his plausible explanation: "Mama'll kill me if I get my cap dirty."

Ha. And that was just one of the hundreds of memories I have of growing up in one of the finest ballparks in all of North Louisiana.

Chapter Four

Reflections

Black Dog

I guess it all hits us from time to time, this thing called depression. It hits me too, but not to the extent it does others. I'll get sad from time to time about something, but it never lasts for very long. Usually some kind words or a pat on the back from a friend helps me through it.

What the medical community calls clinical depression is much more serious, like a sad cold that turns into pneumonia.

Several of my family members and friends suffer from depression. Some have been diagnosed and are being treated. Some have not and need to be. Some are taking Zoloft, Lexapro, or some other depression fighting drugs.

The list of people who have suffered from depression is quite long and varied by profession. It includes political leaders like Abraham Lincoln and Winston Churchill, actors Heath Ledger, Harrison Ford, and Emma Thompson, and musicians Billy Joel, Brian Wilson, and Kurt Cobain.

Actor Owen Wilson's recent attempted suicide was attributed to frequent bouts with depression. Nirvana grunge rocker, Kurt Cobain, was successful in taking his life. They had both reached that point where the happiness scale had become so tilted to one side that it made life seem unbearable and undesirable.

Mike Wallace from *60 Minutes* discussed what it was like to suffer from depression. He said it was like everything that made him happy was buried somewhere in a Mason jar so deep in the ground that he couldn't get to it. Only after he was able to treat his illness with medication could he open "the jar" and find the happiness he'd lost.

Winston Churchill called depression the "black dog." When he found himself feeling the affects he would tell others that "the black dog's in the house." Long before there was a drug like Zoloft, Winnie self-medicated with Scotch to help him keep the black dog a bay.

Let me tell you, when you're trying to help someone who is dealing with depression, you can feel pretty helpless. There's no bleeding to stop, no wound to suture. There's just nothing you can kiss and make feel better.

I'm not a doctor. Ha. I don't even play one on TV. But let me share with you a few dos and don'ts that I've learned about becoming a part of a depression sufferer's support network:

Do

Help them to understand that staying in bed all day or self-medicating is a clear sign that something is wrong
As you would with any other illness, encourage them to seek treatment for theirs
If prescribed, encourage them to stay on their medication
Learn to listen patiently

Don't

Tell them that they should just snap out of it
Tell them that they have nothing to be depressed about
Try to find logic in an illogical mind. To them, they are acting logically
Wait too long

I'll leave you with a piece I wrote some years back about no one in particular, but someone definitely suffering from depression. It's called "Don't Pet the Black Dog."

Black dog stopped by today
Stared at me with not much to say
Then he started bayin' at the moon
Sure sign he won't be leavin' here soon

Locked the door left the key by the bed
To get away from the voices inside my head
Black dog said to pay 'em no mind
Hearing that's a real bad sign

He's here now and he's gonna stay
Black dog ridin' the rest of the way
Dog's in the valley, dog's on the hill
Black dog testin' every inch of my will

Black dog curled up at the foot of my bed
Waitin' to see if I'm living or dead
When you see the black dog, you got the blues
Don't pet the black dog, don't make the front page news

The End of an Era

Here's the question I had to ask myself: If it was lake water instead of alcohol, would the amount I drank in my lifetime come closer to Lake Ponchartrain or Superior? Tough question, but maybe that was one reason I decided to quit drinking. Well, there's that, and the idea that I may need to operate heavy machinery one day.

I haven't missed it that much, and so far, there's been considerable upside to sobriety:

- I no longer have a cab company or a defense attorney on retainer
- My jokes are better now that I can remember the punch line
- I can watch LSU blow a late-game lead without throwing the remote through my TV set

It's fun now to look back at when it all started. Growing up a good Baptist in a dry parish in North Louisiana, of course I didn't drink (either). Drinking was pretty well hidden around where I'm from. It's like that old joke about how Catholics don't recognize Mormons, the Jews don't recognize Jesus, and Baptists don't recognize each other at the liquor store.

I think I first tasted alcohol at the ripe old age of 8 when I came up on Pawpaw Colvin and one of his buddies out in the carport having a snort. Papaw poured a little whiskey in the pint bottle cap, handed it to me, and said, "Here, take a sip."

It tasted like a lit Brillo pad going down and singed my nose hairs. Needless to say, it was not a great first impression. I think Pawpaw probably wanted it that way.

On into my early teenage years I tried Boone's Farm. The FDA should sanction Boone's Farm for its laxative and vomit-inducing qualities, like ipecac. I never saw any of my friends get drunk on that sweet wine, but I saw plenty get sick.

If I wanted a sip, all I had to do was slip a little of my hard earned lawn mowing money into the hands of whatever hoodlum was making a run to Cheniere Inn or Moon's Drive-in.

Most of the time this occurred at a night basketball game in Dubach. Me and the rest of the evildoers never sat inside the gym so our parents could keep an eye on us. We preferred to stay outside and watch the game through the pane glassed windows.

As far as Daddy was concerned, as long as I could tell him the ending score of the game, I could stay outside and plot to overthrow the government. To him, knowing the score meant I was watching the game instead of outside fooling around. Most of the time I could tell him the score but not who we played.

I graduated from high school without much drinking at all. Then I went off to LSU where they give you a pint of bourbon if you can figure out freshman registration.

I like to say that was in the Sigma Chi fraternity at LSU until I got the first bill. Social fraternities at LSU drink a great deal. Kegs of beer were at every function and I remember hearing the "drink chug-a-lug, drink chug-a-lug" chant until my mug was empty.

Then I was on to a career in sales, where constant pressure to meet a monthly quota can lead one to a liquid stress reliever.

I know it sounds like the start of a country song when I say, "So here I am now, dry as a bone, and wondering why it took so long." But then I guess, if you ever drank Lake Ponchartrain, you'd know what I mean. Cheers!

Cross on the Side

I'd much prefer to drive than fly. I see things better when I drive. You can't see unleaded gas going to $5 a gallon when you fly.

I know that airlines are feeling the fuel crunch as well. They're now charging for services we used to get for free. I read the other day where they're going to start charging for soft drinks.

Soon it will cost me more to check my luggage than my luggage is worth.

I've been thinking of some subtle ways I can show my displeasure with the airlines. Maybe the next time the flight attendant goes to hand me a bag of pretzels I could say, "I'll accept those stale pretzels for two dollars and the napkin will cost you 50 cents. Oh and, correct change is appreciated."

I wouldn't be surprised if one day they install those coin locks on the bathroom doors. Then we can hear the captain could come on the intercom and say, "Uh, ladies and gentlemen, we've reached our cruising altitude. I'm going to turn off the seatbelt sign (ding) so please feel free to move about the cabin."

"The pay toilets are located fore and aft. But, if you don't have two solid quarters on you, I wouldn't recommend the spectacular view of Niagara Falls outside the left side of the aircraft."

One of the things I don't enjoy seeing when I drive is those little white crosses on the side of the road.

I know every one of them has a story, one I may never know. That doesn't stop me from wondering how each one of them probably started with a phone call asking someone to come quick to the emergency room, the ICU, or the funeral home.

Most of these crosses appear so simple and white. Sometimes I see more than one with one slightly bigger than the others as if to signify there was an age difference in those who perished.

Who builds these crosses? Who wakes up one morning and goes out to a dewy hill, a bent stop sign, a busy intersection and puts up one or more crosses?

Do these crosses represent the scene of an accident or the point of ascension? Is this where the vehicle occupants died or from whence they rose? I wonder.

Don't they know that people like me more often than not zoom by too fast to pay our proper respects?

Once back during my song writing days, I decided to write a song about all those crosses. It's been recorded by a couple of musicians but never published.

The idea came to me one day while driving home from Ruston on I-20. You can't get much to rhyme with twenty so I changed it to I-95.

It's about a truck driver driving up from Florida who finally decides to stop and check out one of the white crosses along his route.

It's called *Cross on the Side.*

I've traveled this highway time after time
Up from the panhandle along the white lines
North out of Weldon it caught my eye
A cross on the side of I-95

It was a small white cross made of wood
Just feet from the exit alone there it stood
I decided to stop there, I don't even know why
To see a cross on the side of I-95

Chorus

I don't know what happened here
Don't even know your name
When I pass this way again
I won't ever feel the same
Each time I do
I'll thank the Lord that I'm alive
Alive to pass your cross
On the side of I-95

A well-worn path led to the top
Of a little hill where it stopped
It had flowers, but most of them died
At a cross on the side of I-95

Rain-soaked picture lay on the ground
A beaming boy in his cap and his gown
He must have decided to go for a ride
That ended on the side of I-95

A little plastic card read, "From DeeDee and Tom"
"God bless you and keep you, our only son"
With a great deal of sadness I knelt and I cried
At a cross on the side of I-95

Musak to My Ears

Well it looks like my comatose song writing career may have felt a slight twinge in its little finger today. Just when I had started to think I couldn't get Velcro to stick, I got an e-mail from my co-writer Ann Wilson-Hardin up in Lipp Loch, Oklahoma. She said that a publisher had contacted her about getting the rights to one of our songs.

First I had to check the calendar to see if it was April Fool's Day, and it wasn't, so I wrote her back and told her that, while they had already caught the Unabomber, it would be wise to check this guy out to see if he was some wild-eyed maniac living in a super-small cabin up in the mountains.

Another reason I suggested the scrutiny is because, so far, Annie and I have successfully kept our musical talents so well hidden that it would be easier for a publisher to find Jimmy Hoffa.

I think it was Mark Twain who once said, "I wouldn't join a club that would have me as a member." Well, along those same lines, I'm not real sure I want to sign a deal with a publisher who would have me under contract.

Although we've co-written several songs together, Annie and I don't always see eye to eye. Well, let's just say we have our musical differences. Okay, it would be closer to the truth if I said that we get along more like Lenin and McCarthy than the famous Beatles songwriting duo.

When I thought she just might be *the* Ann Wilson, the lead singer for Heart, I contacted Annie over the Internet. Of course, if I'd been thinking, I would have known that Heart's Ann Wilson would never be caught dead in Oklahoma unless she'd been placed there under the witness protection program.

Because I don't play an instrument, typically Annie writes the melody while I write most of the words. One of these days I'm going to teach myself to play the guitar. My brother Benji has a Masters Degree in classical guitar from SMU; so you'd think I could learn a few chords.

But I'm not totally devoid of musical talent. If I can ever find out where Elmo hid my harmonicas, I could still play you a mean version of "Love Me Do." She started hiding them because every time I played the harmonica, my Sheltie dog Miles (named after the jazz great Miles Davis) would howl then bite me on the ankle. She said my playing hurt his ears. I thought it was because he a Rolling Stones fan.

It would be easy to quit trying to break into the music business. Very few do and there's a saying in Nashville that you've got to be present to win. Meaning unless you look and sing like Tim McGraw, don't try and mail in your talent. Come here and starve for a while like the rest of us – pay your dues.

That always sounded fair to me, but since I look more like Boxcar Willie these days than Tim McGraw, I think it's better that I stay put and hold on to my day job a while longer.

I heard another story about how tough it is to break into Nashville: a middle-aged man came over to the table where country music super star Vince Gill and a few of his friends were sitting. He inquired of Vince how he could break into the music business. Vince was cordial with his advice, but after the gentleman walked away, he remarked to his friends, "Don't he know this is a young man's town?"

Not that our age would stop us, I just don't think Annie or I have any plans to move to Nashville. So I guess me and the Queen of Loch Lipp will just have to keep on mailing them in.

Who knows, one day we might get lucky and this new Unapublisher will make us famous!

Let's Commence

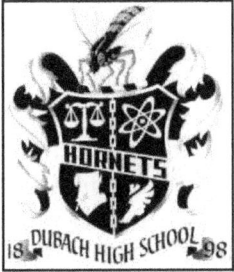

Note: I considered it an honor of a lifetime to be asked to speak to the 2008 graduating class at Dubach High School. Here is a copy of that speech.

First of all, I want to thank Ms. Lala Cooper and Principal Judy Mabry for inviting me here on graduation night to make a few remarks.

Some months ago, when Ms. Cooper invited me to speak, I couldn't help but think about all the Dubach High School teachers of mine who had to pass away in order for me to be up here.

I know that any one of them, if they were still alive, would surely have put their foot down and said, NO, anybody but him. But, oh well; now they're gone, and I'm here.

The first thing I want to do tonight is say something directly to those who are about to graduate. Two things really...

First, you can relax. I know that you can't wait to get out of here. So I've timed my speech and it doesn't take more than an hour and a half to give.

Secondly, and more seriously...I know that you've heard that the 3 most beautiful words in the English language are "I LOVE YOU," Right? But not always...

On graduation night, the 3 words you want to hear are: YOU MADE IT!

Wearing a maroon cap and gown, it was 34 years ago that I sat right where you are tonight. It was 34 years ago that I walked across this stage as an honor graduate of Dubach High School.

We didn't have air conditioning in this gym then and it was hot and I was sweating pretty good. I also remember being scared, scared at the thought of leaving my comfort zone.

Are any of you feeling that right now?

And I had quite a comfort zone. Daddy fixed me breakfast every morning. Sometimes it was just a couple of pieces of toast, maybe some cold cereal or oat meal. But something was always on the table in the morning before school.

Mama made sure I had clean clothes to wear. All I had to do was get up and go to school. Once I got to school, my day was laid out for me too. First I reported to home room, and then attended various classes, maybe a study hall, recess, lunch, PE, then usually something to do after school with sports (baseball or basketball). I just didn't have too much to worry about.

But on the night of my graduation, right here where we are tonight, I was both worried and scared. I was worried about what was going to happen to me from here on out.

The author of the *Power of Positive Thinking*, Norman Vincent Peale, once wrote about how a baby must feel in the womb.

A baby is all warm and comfortable. Then it comes time to be born and the baby thinks, "Wait a minute, I'm all warm and comfortable. Where are you taking me?"

Then the baby comes into the world, looks around, spends a little time, and starts to think, "Hey, this ain't so bad. In fact, I like this. This'll do just fine."

Yet you could never have convinced that baby that, while warm in its womb, that anything outside could be just as good. That baby had to born to find that out. It had to leave one world in order to enter another.

Thirty-four years ago, I was warm and comfortable in my surroundings here. Sitting right where you are, I was waiting to be born of Dubach High School. Just like that baby, like it or not, my time had come.

Scared though I was, it was time for me to enter into another world, into another stage of my life.

The night I walked out of this gym, I had no idea what life had in store for me. But you know what? It wasn't so bad.

All I had to do was remember to honor those who loved me enough to educate me. All I had to do was remember to honor who fixed my breakfast, made sure I had clean clothes to wear, and those who gave me a moral compass to follow. All I had to do was believe in myself and remember that I had been well prepared for life.

It's amazing how much smarter my parents got after I had been out a few years. Once I realized that clothes don't wash themselves, food doesn't magically appear on the table, and that I had to get myself up when the alarm went off…that's when I knew (for sure) that I had been raised by two geniuses.

I saw a movie not too long ago starring Morgan Freeman and Jack Nicholson. It was called *The Bucket List*. One scene in particular had Morgan explaining to Jack how to gain access into Egyptian heaven.

He said you must first answer two questions.

The first question is: Did you find joy in your life?

The second question is: Did you bring joy to the lives of others?

I'd like to take the second question first.
If you recall, I said a minute ago that life after graduation wasn't so bad because I remembered the lessons I was taught. One such lesson came from my mother. She taught me that, for all the things out of our control, there is one thing of which we will always be in control. And that is whether or not to be a kind person.

Did you bring joy to the lives of others?

When your life is over and you're standing at the gates of heaven, don't you want to be able to answer that question yes?

Whether or not you leave here tonight to graduate from Med School or dig ditches for a living is really not as important to society as you might think.

In the end, society will judge you on how well you treated your fellow man. Did you bring joy to the lives of others?

Each one of you will leave here tonight given a piece of paper that (in a way) welcomes you into society. It means you made it.

You will also leave here tonight with a gift God gave you on day one. A gift you were born with. You CAN be kind. You CAN bring joy to the lives of others.

You may have guessed now why I took the second question first. If you can answer (yes) to the second question: did you bring joy to the lives of others?

Then you also have the answer to the first question. If you can bring joy to the lives of others, then you too WILL find joy in YOUR life.

In closing, I want to wish the best of luck to the graduates of Dubach High School. You're following in a long line of those who learned their lessons well.

If you remember to honor the memory of those who taught you those lessons, you will do well in whatever you choose to do.

And a far as tonight goes? YOU MADE IT. Goodnight and may God bless you all.

Light Music

My family was, and still is, full of music lovers. Most of us started at an early age. I'm guessing my big sister Jean was the first one to bring music into our house. She had a little box-shaped monograph record player that had a handle and folded up like an overnight case. I guess that made it easier for her to carry it to teenage sleepovers. Surely they had electricity by then.

By the time she left home for Louisiana Tech, I was old enough to play the 45 RPM records she left behind. I couldn't read the record labels so I just stared at them while they went round and round on the small turn table. That, and growing up a block away from a sewer pond, probably explains a lot about how I turned out to be.

At some point, somebody must have showed me how to stack records so that I could play more than one at a time. After that, I could not only watch the labels spin, I could stare as the little tone arm went to the end of the record then gracefully moved out of the way so the next record could drop. For a kid not yet kindergarten age, this was seriously good stuff

I know that I hadn't yet grasped the concept of who Elvis was or what he meant at the time to the music-loving world. But that didn't keep me from enjoying the hound dog song or the one about him not wanting somebody stepping on his shoes or being cruel to him.

One in the stack was about Mama Kissing Santa Claus. Not my mama, somebody else's mama, 'cause I asked. It was explained to me that sometimes daddies like to dress up like Santa Claus and kiss their wives while they're dressed up like Mrs. Claus.

I don't remember Daddy ever dressing up for anything except for when he would wear a fez to his Masonic lodge meetings. I also don't think I ever heard a song about somebody kissing a Mason around Christmas time or any other time for that matter.

Later on, when I was a moody teenager waiting to see if my hormones were ever going to fly in formation, one of my favorite things to do was go into our living room, close the door, turn off the lights, lie down on the floor with a pillow under my head, and listen to music while staring at the little red light on our family stereo.

I would listen to LPs like Meet the Beatles, Rubber Soul, and Revolver. For Christmas one year I got an 8-track tape player and a Blood Sweat & Tears tape. This meant I could now turn off the lights, assume the position, and watch four lights go click from left to right as the tracks changed. There was just one problem though.

Did you ever read the comic strip Peanuts when Charlie Brown talked about doing battle with the kite-eating tree? Well, I had a tape-eating 8-track.

Right in the middle of a good mid-afternoon groove the music would just stop. I would get up and eject the tape only to find most of it was no longer in the cartridge but stuck inside the player and wrapped around the capstan.

It took the skill of a surgeon to get the tape out without breaking it. Then I had to use a little screwdriver to take the cartridge apart so I could rewind it. The first time I opened up an 8-track tape I was amazed. It went on for 8 miles with two inner circles going in opposite directions. If the tape ever got twisted, the next step was to toss it in the waste basket. I don't do snarled.

Later I put an 8-track in my car. It was the one I could afford at the time - some cheap DynSonic brand. Now I could hear my tapes getting eaten while driving 65 miles an hour.

When ever that would happened, I would roll down my window, say a few choice words, and do my best to hit a deer crossing sign with that no good snarled outfit. One by one that tape-eating car stereo devoured every 8-track tape I had in my shoebox.

I slowly progressed over the years to cassettes, then to CDs and DVDs but nothing ever held my attention the way that little red light did.

Looking back, I think it might have been less about the light and more about how, as a teenager, we needed a way and a place to cope with the sad times that we all went through at that age. I feel fortunate that I had a place to untangle my thoughts. Like I said, I don't do snarled.

I Saw a Lot This Year (Memories of 2007)

I saw a sweet little baby boy come into this world
I saw a friend's young son leave this world
I saw my dear little cousin send her son off to war
I saw good friends go in a different direction
I saw friends comfort their loved ones nearing the end of their journey
I saw young students who were inspired to write and draw
I saw people enjoy the book I wrote for them
I saw my publisher fight his way back to good health
I saw that I really could get off the couch and exercise
I saw Daddy turn 91
I saw some family members get better, get worse, and get on with life
I saw lots of old friends
I saw my old church have its first reunion
I saw that I could leave the spirits and still keep mine
I saw sadness, heartache, and tears
I saw the tears that can also come from joy and happiness
I saw another year go by

But mostly, I saw this as an opportunity to wish you and your family a very merry Christmas and a happy New Year!

The Plant

It would be easier to say who didn't work there than did. Dubach was a company town if there ever was one.

Owned by Southwest Gas then later Kerr-McGee, to the people who worked there and their families it was simply called: "The Plant."

When I was little, Daddy would take me down there and try his best to explain to me what he did for a living. As we walked around, he would point out the pipe farm, the cooling tower, and the tank farm where trucks came to load up on gasoline.

I would always pretend to understand as he described the process for making naphtha or some other petroleum-based product. I was more interested at the prospect of getting a Milky Way and a Coke from the refrigerator in the break room.

After asking me what kind of candy bar I wanted, that's where Daddy would put money in a little cardboard box. That's when I first learned of the term "honor system."

With short mown grass and raked chat gravel, The Plant's grounds were as spotless as an army base. Most of the men who worked there had been in the service during World War II. Maybe that had something to do with it.

That's what my two brothers, Benji and Jimmy, did during high school summers. They mowed, raked chat gravel, and painted The Plant.

Those shining silver processing towers looked like rocket ships piercing the sky.

My oversized hard hat was required wear and I had to hold on tight to it to keep it from falling off my head as I looked up to see if I could see the top of those towers.

Sometimes the noise there was so loud I could hardly hear what Daddy was saying. Nevertheless, I knew to nod and look interested because that might be the difference in my getting to come back sometime. The ability to look interested has served me well into my adult years.

One day The Plant caught fire. I think it had something to do with lightning hitting a tree across the street from the main installation consequently igniting some runoff fuel.

Being a gasoline plant and all, needless to say, that if that fire had gotten across the street to the main facility the town of Dubach would have resembled Hiroshima.

I think I was 12 at the time and remember Daddy coming home just long enough to rinse the soot off, grab something to eat, and return to fight the fire. For obvious reasons, every able bodied man from Southwest Gas was there lending a hand in getting that fire under control. They were all friends and family. They went to company picnics and played on the softball team together. This was in defense of their homes and their livelihoods.

Some years later Southwest Gas was bought out by Kerr-McGee. Shortly after they took over, Daddy was informed that his existing classification didn't exist in their book. So, after 20-something years of service, they would have to bump him down to a classification they did have – that of a roustabout - being paid slightly over minimum wage. Daddy didn't approve of that decision, so he decided to help start a union.

I helped him write the letter that invited the union organizer in. I sat with them at our dinner table one night when he explained to Daddy how the process worked. The vote to unionize was narrow but it passed. Once in, the union reestablished Daddy and his coworker's wages back to their previous levels.

After that, Daddy never felt the same about his work home. It was like big corporate rules and regulations had ruined their little family.

The place they had risked their lives to save from a fire just wasn't the same anymore. Worse than that, he quit taking me down there for a Milky Way and a Coke. That's when I knew it was serious.

The Last Lap

Stock car racing has sure changed a lot since I was a kid growing up in the 60's. I went every year to the stock car races at the Shreveport Fair and had no idea what was going on out there on the track. All I knew was that my internal organs would quake when the cars raced by and that it was so loud I couldn't hear or talk to the person sitting beside me.

My NASCAR friends like Billy Don Knowles will have to forgive me because I don't know what all the flags mean. Well, I know some of the easier ones. There's the checkered one – that signifies someone won – and a yellow one, which means drive with caution because there's been a crash or maybe oil has been spilled somewhere on the track.

So what if they wave the black flag? Does that mean they found roaches? Ha! I'm just kidding Donnie. You can hang up the phone.

The most interesting flag to me is the white one they use to signal the last lap of the race. That seems to me to be when most of the hard decisions have to be made. If you're only a couple of cars back from taking the lead, do you go for it? Do you attempt the move that might get you the lead or just lay back and settle for what you've got?

I just turned 52 this past January. I can relate to the concept of the last lap. Of course, we don't get the benefit of a waved flag to tell us when we're in it. We don't know how the long the lap will be. My dad retired over 25 years ago. Now in his 90's, his last lap has lasted for a good long time.

Some call it a mid-life crisis when a fifty or sixty-something buys a red Corvette or a Harley and lets their hair down a little. What's wrong with that? Why should it be considered a crisis? I think the crisis would be in knowing you were in your last lap and not running it the way you want. As it should be, how long our final lap will last is out of our hands. Given good health, how we choose to run the final lap is well within our control.

I always said that there are three things you should get out of if you're miserable. (Now remember that I said miserable and not just inconvenienced) One is a job, the other is a relationship, and the third is a mattress. The reason for that is you spend way too much of your life in all three. Life's too short for any one of them to be making you miserable.

When I look back on how I've lived my life to date, there's nothing I can do to change it. Are there things I would, if I could? Sure. Who wouldn't? Not knowing if my last lap will be, like my father's, 40 years or closer to 40 days is fine with me. I don't want to know that much. What I want to know is, however long the last lap is, that it will be run the right way.

The idea of my having one last lap is something to celebrate, something exciting, not something to fear. It means it's time to become more focused on getting the best out the years remaining, that's all. There's no crisis, nothing morbid, or anything wrong with that. It's a healthy state of mind.

You may not see me behind the wheel of red Corvette or on the seat of a Harley. That's not something I long to do. What you will see me doing is enjoying this last lap for as long as it lasts. I plan to run each day at top speed while always keeping an eye out for the yellow flag.

At times I may choose to hang back a little and just enjoy the ride. One day I may just decide that it's time to go for it, whatever go for it means.

Either way, here's hoping there's a checkered flag at the end.

Cheers! Randy

INDEX

How to Order

The Second Pine Cone Collection

Cost $20.00 per copy
Add $8 for shipping and handling

U.S. mail:

Please send your payment and mailing address to:

> Randy Rogers
> 1724 Huron Trail
> Plano, Texas 75075

Ordering via E-mail:

Dubachdaddy@yahoo.com subject line "Book Order"

Ordering by Phone or Voice Mail:

972-516-6658.

Note: If you would like a signed copy or one to give as a gift, please indicate that on your order and how you would like it to read.

For general comments or ideas for a story?

Dubachdaddy@yahoo.com

www.ingramcontent.com/pod-product-compliance
Lightning Source LLC
Chambersburg PA
CBHW021343090426
42742CB00008B/731